Object-Oriented Type Systems

Object-Oriented Type Systems

Jens Palsberg and Michael I. Schwartzbach
Aarhus University, Denmark

JOHN WILEY & SONS
Chichester · New York · Brisbane · Toronto · Singapore

Other Wiley Editorial Offices

John Wiley & Sons, Inc., 605 Third Avenue,
New York, NY 10158-0012, USA

Jacaranda Wiley Ltd, G.P.O. Box 859, Brisbane,
Queensland 4001, Australia

John Wiley & Sons (Canada) Ltd, 22 Worcester Road,
Rexdale, Ontario M9W 1L1, Canada

John Wiley & Sons (SEA) Pte Ltd, 37 Jalan Pemimpin #05-04,
Block B, Union Industrial Building, Singapore 2057

British Library Cataloguing in Publication Data

A catalogue record for this book is available from the British
Library

ISBN 0 471 94128 X

Produced from camera-ready copy supplied by the authors
Printed and bound in Great Britain by Biddles Ltd, Guildford
and King's Lynn

Contents

Preface

Type systems are required to ensure reliability and efficiency of software. For object-oriented languages, typing is an especially challenging problem because of inheritance, assignment, and late binding. Existing languages employ different type systems, and it can be difficult to compare, evaluate, and improve them, since there is currently no uniform theory for such languages.

This book provides such a theory. We review the type systems of SIMULA, SMALLTALK, C++, and EIFFEL and we present a type system that generalizes and explains all of them.

Chapter 1 contains a summary of the book. We survey the problems faced by the designer of an object-oriented type system and we review existing solutions (Chapter 2). We then define an idealized language which will be the basis for our theory (Chapter 3). This language, called BOPL (Basic Object Programming Language), contains common features of SIMULA, SMALLTALK, C++, and EIFFEL. For BOPL we provide a type system (Chapter 4), a type inference algorithm (Chapter 5), and a study of the typing of inheritance (Chapter 6) and genericity (Chapter 7).

This book is intended as a supplementary text for a course on object-oriented programming. We have ourselves used this book in a fourth year course at Aarhus University. Half of the lectures were spent on covering this book, half on covering other material. We have also given half-day tutorials on the material in this book, at OOPSLA'92, ECOOP'93, and OOPSLA'93.

We thank our editor at Wiley, Gaynor Redvers-Mutton, for enthusiastic support. We also thank the students of our Spring 1993 course for many helpful comments and suggestions for exercises. Finally, we thank Peter Juhl for his careful proofreading and many insightful remarks.

Århus, July 1993

Jens Palsberg
Michael I. Schwartzbach

How to Use This Book

This book is intended as a supplementary text for a one-semester advanced undergraduate or introductory graduate course on object-oriented programming. The book is accompanied by a freely available workbench with implementations of all algorithms. For details of how to get and how to use the workbench, see Appendix B.

The book requires a basic understanding of object-oriented programming and is otherwise self-contained. Covering the material in this book will require about half of a one-semester course. There are several possibilities for the remaining part of the course. One is to let the course be on selected topics in object-oriented programming with type systems being one of them. Here are a few others:

- A study of object-oriented type systems. In this case, the book presents a coherent theory that explains the common features of major languages.
- A detailed presentation of a specific object-oriented language. In this case, the book provides a framework for evaluating the type system of the language, as well as a source of information about other languages.
- A survey of several object-oriented languages. In this case, the book provides a structured setting for comparing their type systems.
- Programming projects. The source code of the workbench, see Appendix B, is a natural basis for programming explorations.

Each chapter contains several exercises and bibliographical notes providing suggestions for further reading. Solutions to selected exercises and at least 100 slides on the material in this book can be obtained by anonymous *ftp* from the machine:

daimi.aau.dk   (130.225.16.1)

in the directory:

pub/oots/doc

See the README file for further details.

All questions, comments, errata, etc., can be sent to us at oots@daimi.aau.dk.

1

Introduction

This chapter gives a quick summary of the book.

1.1 Object-Oriented Languages and Type Systems

In Chapter 2 we recall the ideas of typing and object-oriented programming and we summarize the typing problems that are specific to object-oriented languages. As a basis for the remainder of the book, we then review existing solutions to these problems, both those found in SIMULA, SMALLTALK, C++, and EIFFEL, and also those given in theoretical work based on the λ-calculus.

1.2 The BOPL Language

In Chapter 3 we introduce and motivate the BOPL language. BOPL is an idealized untyped object-oriented language that contains common features of SIMULA, SMALLTALK, C++, and EIFFEL. The main features of BOPL are classes, objects, assignments, and late binding. In the remainder of the book we provide a type system and a type inference algorithm for BOPL, and we study extensions with inheritance and genericity.

1.3 A Variety of Languages

We have deliberately designed BOPL so that it is untyped and does not feature inheritance or genericity. This enables us to gradually introduce these constructs. In total, we will study eight languages, as illustrated in the following table.

		Inheritance	Genericity	Inheritance+Genericity
Untyped	BOPL	IBOPL	SBOPL	ISBOPL
Typed	TBOPL	ITBOPL	STBOPL	ISTBOPL

A language can be typed or untyped, it can feature inheritance, and it can feature genericity. This yields $2 \times 2 \times 2 = 8$ languages. All eight languages have BOPL as their kernel. For the syntax of the languages, see Appendix A.

We use the letter T for *typed*, I for *inheritance*, and S for *genericity*. The last of these may seem odd, but the genericity mechanism for BOPL will be called *class substitution*, so it is S for *substitution*.

1.4   Program Transformations

Chapters 4–7 contain algorithms for type checking, type inference, etc. We will present *all* the algorithms as *program transformations*, between the eight languages introduced above. The following graph gives an overview of the algorithms and thus of the rest of the book. The graph does not mention IBOPL and ITBOPL, to keep the illustration simple.

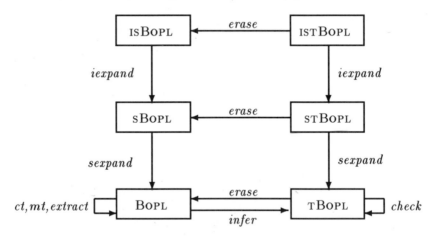

A *program transformation* is a function from one program text to another in essentially the same language. Thus, it defines a syntactic rewriting of programs. Our program transformations will be *semantics preserving*, that is, the transformed program has the same semantics as the original program. This may appear to be of quite limited use, since the transformation leaves the behavior unchanged. However, the transformed program might differ from the original in efficiency or in the style in which it is written. For example, the type inference algorithm produces as a typed program from an untyped one. We now give a brief overview of the program transformations.

- The three *erase* transformations are most easily understood. They simply erase all type annotations and thus change a typed program into an equivalent untyped version.

- The *iexpand* and *sexpand* transformations remove all uses of inheritance and class substitution by rewriting them in terms of simpler mechanisms. Such expansions may drastically increase the size of a program, which emphasizes the succinctness that is gained by powerful programming concepts. The two transformations are identical for the typed and untyped versions of the language.
- The *check* transformation type checks a typed program. It is a program transformation because it inserts run-time type checks if the program is not statically type correct. This can only modestly increase the size of a program.
- The *infer* transformation produces a typed program from an untyped one. The optimal type information is of course uncomputable, so *infer* can only produce a conservative approximation.
- The *ct* and *mt* transformations support the type inference algorithm. If one or more applications of these transformations precede *infer*, then the computed type information can be considerably more precise. Both transformations work by copying code, thereby allowing the code to be analyzed separately in a different contexts. Specifically, *ct* copies classes and *mt* copies methods. Each application may drastically increase the size of a program.
- The *extract* transformation removes dead code. It is of course undecidable if a piece of code is dead, so *extract* will in some cases leave some dead code in the resulting program.

Each time we introduce a new concept, it will lead to the presentation of one of these program transformations.

All the algorithms are implemented in a workbench which is freely available. For details, see Appendix B.

1.5 Type Checking

Chapter 2 contains a discussion of the requirements for an object-oriented type system. In Chapter 4 we present a simple yet general type system that meets these requirements. In this type system, types are sets of classes.

The idea behind these types is that if an expression has type {A,B,C}, then it can only evaluate to nil or to instances of class A, B, or C. Stating such invariants by means of explicit type annotations may improve the readability of programs and if the invariants are valid, then they can also help improve reliability and efficiency.

We use a constraint based technique to define the static type correctness of programs. We introduce a type variable $[\![E]\!]$ for every expression E. These type variables are related through various type constraints that soundly reflect

the semantics of the different programming constructs. For example, the
constraints for an assignment are:

$$[\![x]\!] \supseteq [\![x{:}{=}E]\!] = [\![E]\!]$$

whereas:

$$[\![\text{if } E_1 \text{ then } E_2 \text{ else } E_3 \text{ end}]\!] = [\![E_2]\!] \cup [\![E_3]\!]$$

$$[\![E_1]\!] \subseteq \{\text{Bool}\}$$

capture the meaning of conditionals.

The values of some of these type variables are given by the explicit type
annotations. This is true of those for instance variables, formal arguments,
and method bodies.

We define static correctness of a program to be satisfiability of its type
constraints. This is checked by an algorithm that implicitly generates the
constraints systematically from the syntax and attempts to satisfy them.

As always, static correctness is a decidable property that conservatively
approximates the genuinely undecidable validity of the type invariants. Thus,
a program may be statically incorrect even though its type invariants are in
fact valid. However, if a program is deemed statically correct, then validity of
the type invariants is guaranteed. An example of the inherent imprecision can
be seen in the constraints for conditionals, where it is pessimistically assumed
that both branches will always be evaluated and thus contribute to the type
of the result.

If a program is not statically correct, then it can always be transformed
into a corresponding one that is. The idea is to insert a dynamic type check
at all message sends, just like what is done in SMALLTALK implementations.
We will present a better algorithm that inserts much fewer dynamic checks.

Our type system is a generalization of the type systems of SIMULA, C++,
and EIFFEL. The reason is that our type rules are phrased for arbitrary sets,
whereas class types can only specify certain sets. We will demonstrate how to
specialize the general type rules to rules for class types.

1.6   Type Inference

Chapter 4 defines static type correctness as the question of whether the
explicit type annotations satisfy some type constraints. In Chapter 5 we
remove the type annotations and do type inference by solving the remaining
constraints.

We do not want to flatly reject programs that cannot be annotated to
yield static type correctness. There are good pragmatic reasons for that:
applications involving for example heterogeneous collections, simply cannot be

written without such checks, unless unsafe assignments are silently accepted as in C++. We will compute a reasonable annotation and then let the type checking algorithm in Chapter 4 insert a minimal number of dynamic checks.

Object-oriented programs often use polymorphic methods and heterogeneous collections. Our type inference algorithm cannot deal well with such ones. The result is that a type check that follows type inference may insert disappointingly many dynamic type checks. Fortunately, it is possible to generate more precise constraints, which are also somewhat more complicated. We will use a combination of two techniques.

The first improvement is to consider the existence of "dead code", i.e., code that can never be executed in the current application. This is a particularly common thing in object-oriented programming, where applications may use a large class library containing numerous perhaps unrelated classes. We present an algorithm that can successfully weed out dead code by ensuring that a method is only considered if it can potentially be invoked by a chain of message sends from the main application.

The second improvement comes from the realization that pieces of code may be used in different contexts where they should be given different type annotations. We will present two algorithms that effectively improve the typings of polymorphic methods and heterogeneous collections.

The algorithms for improving inferred types can be iterated. This is especially important for a language like SELF where many methods are polymorphic.

1.7 Inheritance

Inheritance is recognized as a fundamental construct in object-oriented programming. One can for example view it as the basis for a programming methodology where classes are constructed in a conceptual hierarchy. One can also view it as a convenient mechanism for reuse of code.

In Chapter 6 we study a version of inheritance similar to one used in SMALLTALK. We explain the semantics of inheritance as a program transformation. The idea is to transform a program which uses inheritance into one that does not. Thus, starting with an inheritance hierarchy, we produce an equivalent collection of unrelated classes. This explanation of inheritance is convenient for studying typing issues. Towards the end of the chapter, we demonstrate how to implement inheritance such that already compiled code need not be type checked or compiled again.

Not all inheritance hierarchies are legal. We impose a well-formedness condition that is based on the notion of **is-a** and **has-a** relationships. A hierarchy may be viewed as graph, in which every class is a node. There is an **is-a** edge from every subclass to its superclass. Similarly, there is a **has-**

a edge from every class to any other class mentioned in its implementation. The hierarchy is well-formed if no cycle in this graph contains an **is-a** edge. This is a criterion that corresponds well with restrictions imposed in other languages.

The inheritance expansion algorithm applies to well-formed hierarchies. It involves copying and renaming of methods, as well as elimination of **super**. The important typing issue is "what to do about recursion?". Should a subclass of a recursive class be similarly recursive, or should it simply refer to the superclass? We argue that the recursive structure should always be preserved, unless the contrary is explicitly stated. Our expansion algorithm properly reflects this.

Some languages have special features allowing *single* recursion to be preserved, for example the **like Current** in EIFFEL. No language offers solutions for *mutual* recursion, however. With our well-formedness requirement, static type correctness is preserved in subclasses.

1.8   Genericity

Genericity offers a kind of reuse different from inheritance. It is often realized through parameterized classes, although this mechanism has a somewhat uneasy relationship with object-oriented programming. The problem is the need for introducing two kinds of classes, ordinary and parameterized, which do not interact in a satisfying manner. For example, the generic instantiations of a parameterized class do not become subclasses. Also, generic instantiation, unlike inheritance, can only happen once.

In Chapter 7, we compare the genericity mechanisms of EIFFEL, C++, and BETA. The outcome is a suggestion for a new mechanism, called *class substitution*. It views generic instances as subclasses on equal footing with those generated from inheritance. Thus, inheritance and genericity become complementary mechanism, which can even be shown to be orthogonal, i.e., neither can emulate the other. Class substitution makes sense even in an untyped language. A class substitution looks like:

$$C[A_1, A_2 \leftarrow B_1, B_2]$$

This specifies a subclass of class C in which all occurrences of the class A_i has been replaced by the subclass B_i. Such a specification is not realized by a naïve textual substitution. Rather, the substitution algorithm computes a closed set of consequences necessary to preserve static type correctness and implement them all. As for inheritance, we define a well-formedness criterion for programs that use class substitution.

Bibliographical Notes

The idea of explaining part of an implementation by program transformations is known from functional programming, see for example the work of Nielson and Nielson [47, 46]. Program transformations in the realm of object-oriented programming were employed by Bergstein [3] and Casais [13] to obtain better class library organizations.

Exercises

1. Insert IBOPL and ITBOPL into the graph in Section 1.4.
2. Read Appendix B and try out the BOPL workbench.

2

Object-Oriented Languages and Type Systems

This chapter introduces the idea of typing; introduces object-oriented programming; reviews briefly the object-oriented languages of SIMULA, SMALLTALK, C++, and EIFFEL; summarizes the typing problems that are specific to object-oriented languages; discusses the strengths and weaknesses of several known type systems for object-oriented languages; and motivates a basic object-oriented programming language, which we call BOPL, that will be used in the remainder of the book.

2.1 Type Systems

When writing a program, we are interested in making it:

- readable;
- reliable; and
- efficient.

In all three cases, a type system can help. This section explains why and how.

2.1.1 Types are Invariants

Type systems for different programming languages vary markedly. In most cases, however, a type is an *invariant*. Consider for example a variable v from a program in an imperative language. If this variable will contain only integer values in all program executions, then we may say that v has type Integer. The meaning of this statement is that it is an invariant property of all states encountered during execution that the variable v contains an integer value. A reasonable syntax for declaring the variable could be:

       var v: Integer

The annotation "Integer" specifies explicitly the invariant.

A key issue when designing a type system is to choose the possible annotations. If we consider a programming language with only integer and floating-point values, then we may only need two annotations, **Integer** and **Float**. Other languages may involve, for example, structured values and then more complicated annotations are required.

It is of course possible to annotate in a way that does *not* yield an invariant. If, for example, a floating-point value is stored in a variable, then the annotation **Integer** does not specify a valid invariant for that variable. A program in which all type annotations are valid invariants is said to be *type correct*.

It is desirable to make type annotations intelligible for the language implementation. The part of an implementation that deals with types is called a type checker. Its task is to verify that a program is type correct. Ideally, this takes place *before* the program is run. For all but trivial type annotations, however, is it formally undecidable if they specify valid invariants. Thus, a type checker must reject some type correct programs.

If a type checker can statically verify that a program is type correct, then the program is said to be *statically* type correct (with respect to that type checker). Static type correctness implies that all annotations are valid invariants; the reverse implication is false.

An alternative to static type checking is to verify the type correctness while the program is running. If an implementation can do that, then the program is said to be *dynamically* type correct (with respect to that implementation).

Consider for example the program:

```
var v: Integer
v := 7
```

Even a simple type checker can verify that only integer values will be stored in the variable v. Thus, the program is statically type correct. As another example, consider the program:

```
var v: Integer
v := 0;
if v=0 then v := 1 else v := 3.1415 end
```

Clearly, the program is type correct, but many type checkers will be unable to verify this. Thus, with a standard type checker this program is not statically type correct. If we perform straightforward dynamic type checking, however, then clearly we will find that the program is dynamically type correct when executed.

There is a trade-off between static and dynamic type checking. Some type systems offer possibilities for type annotations that make static type checking slow or even impossible. In such cases, it may be advantageous to do dynamic type checking instead, or perhaps to do a combination of static and dynamic type checking.

2.1.2   The Benefits of Types

The invariants stated by type annotations are helpful for making a program:

- readable: types provide documentation,
        "Well-typed programs are more readable";
- reliable: types provide a safety guarantee,
        "Well-typed programs cannot go wrong"; and
- efficient: types enable optimizations,
        "Well-typed programs are faster".

In the following, we take a closer look at these three benefits of types: documentation, safety, and optimization.

First, suppose we are writing a program for adding matrices. We decide to write it as a function with arguments x and y, so in outline it could look like this:

```
function plus(x,y)
  – Code for plus
end
```

Having completed the programming, we decide to somehow document the program. This will be helpful both if we later want to remember what the function is doing and also if somebody else should want to use the function, for example if it becomes part of a library. One option is to make explicit in the *name* of the function that it can add matrices:

```
function matrix-plus(x,y)
  – Code for plus
end
```

Perhaps we should also let the name tell how the matrices should be represented? Such speculation may lead to long names! Another option is to use type annotations:

```
function plus(x,y: Matrix)
  – Code for plus
end
```

Thus, we stick to the short name for the function and instead state explicitly that x and y have to be matrices. In other words, we want this function to be used only if it is an invariant that x and y assume only matrix values. If Matrix is the name of another piece of program text where the representation of matrices is defined, then that is a good place to look for more information. Such search for information could be aided by a programming environment that allows convenient browsing.

The safety aspect of types may be the most important. In most programming languages there are basic operations, like +, which are supposed to work properly only for certain values. For example, it will usually be undefined what is the result of:

    true + 3.1415

In this simple case it is easy to see that the program is meaningless, but for most programming languages it is in general undecidable. Usually, meaningless program parts lead to run-time errors. Of course, it need not be disastrous to have meaningless parts in a program—provided that they are never executed! A program that cannot lead to run-time errors is said to be *safe*. Consider then the following program:

    var x,y: Integer
    . . .
    x + y

Since the variables x and y are annotated with the type Integer, we can guarantee that if the program is type correct, then the addition of x and y is meaningful, although it may still give an exception for e.g. overflow. Notice that the invariant for x and y makes it possible to deduce an invariant for their sum: it is an integer.

For many programming languages it has been a design criterion that:

• the type system should allow all programs to be statically type checked; and
• if a program is type correct, then it is safe.

In other words, it is considered fundamental to enable a compiler to issue a safety guarantee for a program—before that program is run.

In most programming languages, types are important when generating code. Consider for example the following program fragment:

    var r: **record**
            x: Boolean
            y: Integer
        end
    . . .
    r.y := 42

Here the type of r tells the compiler that r will always contain values that have exactly a boolean component named x and an integer component named y.

Thus, we can represent the record in the usual way (as consecutive chunks of storage) and generate efficient code for r.y (with static computation of offsets). Without type information about r, it is likely that we had to choose a more costly representation of r, presumably yielding less efficient code for r.y.

So far, we have considered type information that is written explicitly in the program text. For some type systems, however, it is possible to *omit* the type annotations and let a *type inference* algorithm compute them. Such type systems are said to be *implicit*. Usually, a type inference algorithm submits the computed information directly to other parts of the compiler, rather than explicitly inserting type annotations into the program.

Implicit type systems do not provide the documentation offered by explicit type systems. But if a type inference algorithm is available, then the safety and optimization benefits are the same as if the type annotations were written by the programmer.

It is well-understood how to provide type systems for imperative and functional languages. Usually, the type systems for imperative languages are explicit, as witnessed by PASCAL and ADA. In contrast, there is a tradition for implicit type systems in functional languages such as ML and MIRANDA. There is far less understanding, let alone consensus, on how to provide type systems for object-oriented languages.

2.1.3   World Assumptions

The compilation of a program can happen under various underlying *world assumptions*, and we shall distinguish between two of them.

- The *closed-world* assumption. All parts of the program are known at the time of compilation. In other words, it will not have to be linked together with other modules or libraries. Type checking is done globally for the entire program.
- The *open-world* assumption. The program is divided into independent modules or libraries, which can be compiled separately. Type checking is done locally for each module.

There is no conflict between these two views. Both are reasonable at different stages of the program development process. During the initial explorations, sketches of different parts of the program are prototyped. These may not even be type correct, but it is still useful to be able to execute them to observe their behavior. Often interpreters are most suitable for this stage. Libraries containing off-the-shelf software are commonly employed, and it will certainly save time to have these be previously type checked and compiled. When a finished product has matured, it makes sense to adopt the closed-world assumption, since it enables more advanced compilation techniques. Only when the entire program is known, is it possible to perform global register allocation, flow analysis, or dead code detection. Throughout, we will be careful about these assumptions and their influence on type rules.

Having now presented the idea of type systems, we proceed to a brief introduction to object-oriented programming.

2.2   Object-Oriented Programming

Object-oriented programming is becoming widespread. Numerous programming languages supporting object-oriented concepts are in use, and theories about object-oriented design and implementation are being developed and applied.

A key issue in object-oriented programming is to obtain *reusable* software components. This is achieved through the notions of *object, class, inheritance,* and *late binding,* together with the imperative constructs of *variables* and *assignments.* This section explains why and how these concepts are helpful. In the examples, we will use a convenient syntax that is not supposed to resemble any particular programming language. The constructs that we discuss are not common to all object-oriented languages. Several design alternatives are discussed in the subsequent section.

2.2.1   Terminology

Although some of the notions used in object-oriented programming are specific to that approach, other concepts are borrowed from alternative paradigms. Those concepts that are known from other paradigms are sometimes denoted otherwise than usual. The following table gives a translation of common keywords.

OO-jargon	PASCAL-lingo
object	module
class	module template
instance variable	module variable
method	procedure
message	procedure name
message send	procedure call

The concepts of inheritance and late binding are specific to object-oriented programming. They are the key to the development of reusable software components. In the following we gradually introduce these concepts, starting with plain objects in the form of modules, and then extending with classes, inheritance, and late binding.

2.2.2 Objects

In languages like PASCAL, variables and procedures are separate entities. It is often the case, however, that they can be grouped together in a natural manner. This relationship can be made explicit by means of *abstract data types* or *modules*. For example, a stack can be written as follows.

```
module Stack
    var s: array[1..n] of Element;
    var high: 0..n;

    procedure Init
        high := 0
    end;

    procedure Push(x: Element)
        high := high+1;
        s[high] := x
    end Push;

    procedure Pop: Element
        high := high-1;
        return s[high+1]
    end
end
```

The variables s and high are grouped with the procedures Init, Push, and Pop. The procedures are accessed as Stack.Init, etc. The variables can *not* be accessed from the outside. In object-oriented programming terminology, these kinds of modules are called *objects*.

2.2.3 Classes

There is one obvious problem with the above scenario. If we want *two* instances of a stack, then we must write another identical object. This leads to the idea of *classes*. A class is a *template* for such objects: its instances are objects. The stack example now looks as follows.

```
class Stack
    var s: array[1..n] of Element;
    var high: 0..n;

    method Init
        high := 0
    end;
```

```
method Push(x: Element)
   high := high+1;
   s[high] := x
end Push;

method Pop: Element
   high := high-1;
   return s[high+1]
end
end
```

Notice that procedures are now called *methods*. Two instances of Stack are obtained as:

```
S1 := Stack new;
S2 := Stack new
```

The procedures are accessed as S1.Init and S2.Pop. Here, S1 and S2 are said to be *receivers* of the *messages* Init and Pop. In the implementation, code for the procedures is only generated once. An object contains independently allocated space for the variables.

So far, this could be emulated in PASCAL by the use of records and an extra parameter, as follows.

```
type Stack = pointer to record
                        s: array[1..n] of Element;
                        high: 0..n
             end

procedure Push(self: Stack, x: Element)
   self^.high := self^.high+1;
   self^.s[self^.high] := x
end;

S1 := Stack new; S2 := Stack new
```

Clearly, the syntax with classes is vastly more convenient. However, when we introduce the notion of *inheritance*, the modeling with records is no longer viable.

2.2.4   Inheritance

Consider an extended stack, in which we also want a method Top. Inheritance is a convenient shorthand for defining such as class, since it allows the definition of a class as a modification of another. Thus, we could write:

```
class TopStack inherits Stack
  method Top: Element
    return s[high]
  end
end
```

Instances of TopStack also support all the operations of Stack and inherit all of its variables. We call Stack the *parent* of TopStack. Moreover, Stack is said to be a *superclass* of TopStack, and TopStack is said to be a *subclass*. Both variables and methods can be added in a subclass.

Suppose next that we want a variation of the stack, where it is possible to undo the last Pop operation. We will then write:

```
class UndoStack inherits Stack
  var last: Element;

  method Pop: Element
    last := s[high];
    high := high−1;
    return last
  end;

  method Undo
    high := high+1;
    s[high] := last
  end
end
```

The definition of Pop in UndoStack overwrites the previous definition in Stack.

Inside an object, the meta-variable self refers to the object itself. Another meta-variable, super, is used to gain access to overwritten definitions. For example, UndoStack could be written in the following, more structured manner.

```
class UndoStack inherits Stack
  var last: Element;

  method Pop: Element
    last := s[high]; return super.Pop
  end;

  method Undo
    self.Push(last)
  end
end
```

Inheritance can take place in arbitrarily many levels. Thus, one can obtain a tree-shaped hierarchy of classes, yielding both organizational benefits and considerable code reuse. Many attempts to formalize the program development process have been focused on describing a proper way of organizing such hierarchies.

2.2.5   Late Binding

Object-oriented programming obtains its significance from the combination of inheritance and *late binding*. Late binding means that a message send is dynamically bound to an implementation depending on the class of the receiver.

Suppose for example that we push some objects onto the stack. These objects need not be instances of the same class, but could for example belong to a family of geometric classes such as Circle, Rectangle, or Triangle. Let us assume that they all have a Print method, although these methods may have different implementations for the various classes. At some point we retrieve the top element of the stack and want to print it. Because of late binding, all we need is to send the Print message to the object:

```
var x: Element;
var ts: TopStack;

x := ts.top;
x.Print
```

The implementation of x.Print will then dynamically select the implementation of Print that belongs to the object stored in x.

The combination of inheritance and late binding yields considerable pragmatic advantages. Suppose for example that the classes of geometric objects from before have Print methods that involve identical code to initialize the drawing pad. This code can be placed in a common superclass, Geometric:

```
class Geometric
   method Print
      − Common code for printing geometrical objects
   end
end

class Circle inherits Geometric
   method Print
      ... super.Print ...
   end
end
```

Whenever a new subclass of Geometric is programmed, the existing code in Geometric can readily be exploited.

2.3   Object-Oriented Languages

There is a wide variety of object-oriented languages. This section gives a brief overview of the history of a few prominent languages, and it emphasizes some of the differences between them.

2.3.1   SIMULA

The first object-oriented language is SIMULA. It was developed in the 1960s as an extension of ALGOL-60, and it introduced the notions of object, class, inheritance, and late binding. A major motivation for creating SIMULA was to obtain a language that was well suited for programming of simulations.

SIMULA allows classes to be nested arbitrarily and it has constructs for inspecting the class of an object at run-time. Objects are not encapsulated: variables are accessible from other objects.

Methods can be overwritten, but there is no pseudo-variable super. Instead, there is a construct called inner that allows the original method to call the overwriting method. This ensures that the original code is always executed, thus yielding a weak form of behavior preservation.

The language BETA is a successor of SIMULA. It was developed in the 1970s and it generalizes and streamlines some of the concepts from SIMULA. Notably, it unifies the constructs of class and method into one construct, called a *pattern*.

Both SIMULA and BETA are explicitly typed languages. A type is a class name (in BETA: a pattern name) or an ALGOL-60 type. All variables, formal parameters, and formal result parameters must be annotated with a type. As an example, consider the UndoStack, written in SIMULA:

```
Stack class UndoStack
begin
   ref (Element) last;

   Element procedure Pop
   begin
      last :- s(high);
   end
```

```
    procedure Undo;
    begin
      Push(last)
    end
  end UndoStack
```

Here, Element is the name of a class and last is a variable whose content must be either an instance of Element or a subclass of Element. The new implementation of Pop assumes that the version in Stack was written as:

```
  Element procedure Pop
  begin
    inner;
    high := high−1;
    return s(high+1)
  end
```

Notice the foresight required in placing the inner statement.

Although such type annotations can be statically type checked, SIMULA has chosen a more liberal combination of static and dynamic type checking. To understand why, consider the following program fragment.

```
    class A ...
    A class B ...
    ...
    ref (A) a;
    ref (B) b;
    ...
    a :− b;
    ...
    b :− a;
```

The variable a must refer to instances of A or subclasses of A, and the variable b must refer to instances of B or subclasses of B. Since B is a subclass of A, the assignment a :− b is statically type correct. The assignment b :− a is not statically type correct, however, since a may refer to an instance of A. This assignment may very well be dynamically correct, so instead of rejecting the program, the assignment is dynamically type checked.

2.3.2   SMALLTALK

SMALLTALK was developed in the 1970s. It is inspired by SIMULA, and it is based on taking the notion of *object* as the sole programming metaphor. A major motivation for creating SMALLTALK was to obtain a language that was well suited for graphics programming and that could be the basis for an advanced personal computing environment.

In SMALLTALK, everything is an object. Even classes are objects—instantiated from so-called *meta-classes*. This allows SMALLTALK to structure *all* code in the system, including compilers and debuggers, into a single class hierarchy. One effect of this is that applications in SMALLTALK are intermingled with the rest of the SMALLTALK system. In practice, it is sometimes desirable to extract an application from a SMALLTALK class hierarchy, for example when shipping a product. This turns out to be non-trivial.

SMALLTALK introduced the notions of **self** and **super**, and it enables user-defined control structures, through the use of *blocks*. A block is a suspended computation, akin to the *thunks* used to implement call-by-name in ALGOL-60.

SMALLTALK is a dynamically typed language. No type annotations are written in programs, and only when a message is sent to an object at run-time is it checked if this is well-defined.

The language SELF is a successor of SMALLTALK. It has no class construct: objects are described directly in the program text. SELF features multiple and dynamic inheritance. Multiple inheritance means that an object may have more than one superclass, and dynamic inheritance means that the superclasses may vary at run-time.

2.3.3   C++

C++ was developed in the 1980s. It is inspired by SIMULA and is an extension of C.

In contrast to SIMULA, C++ does not have constructs for inspecting the class of an object at run-time. This allows C++ compilers to use the same storage layout for C++ objects that is used by C compilers for *structs*.

Like SIMULA, C++ is explicitly typed. A type is a class name or a C type. The program fragment with classes **A** and **B** that was presented in the section on SIMULA looks as follows in C++.

```
class A ...
class B : public A ...
...
A *a;
B *b;
...
a = b;
...
b = a;
```

Both assignments are allowed by the compiler but, in contrast to SIMULA, the second assignment is not dynamically type checked! The reason is that this is considered too time demanding.

The language OBJECTIVE-C is another object-oriented extension of C. In contrast to C++, the object-oriented parts of OBJECTIVE-C are dynamically typed, like SMALLTALK programs.

2.3.4 EIFFEL

EIFFEL was developed in the 1980s. Like SIMULA and C++, EIFFEL is explicitly typed. A type is a class name or a predefined type, such as Integer. The program fragment with classes A and B that has been presented in SIMULA and C++ looks as follows in EIFFEL.

```
class A ...
class B ... inherit A ...
...
a: A;
b: B;
...
a := b;
...
b := a;
```

In contrast to SIMULA and C++, the second assignment is illegal in EIFFEL. The programmer has to explicitly insert a dynamic type check of a.

2.4   Class Types

This section develops a common basis for understanding the type systems of the languages that were discussed in the previous section.

The type systems of SIMULA, C++, and EIFFEL are remarkably similar. In all three cases, there are two parts of the type system:

- a *basic* part, which enables the typing of values that are *not* objects, for example integers; and
- an *object-oriented* part, which allows the typing of objects.

The basic parts are somewhat different and depends of course on what kind of non-object values the languages provide. SIMULA and EIFFEL allow types like Integer and Boolean, and C++ allows all C types, including array-types.

The object-oriented parts of the three type systems are similar. To type objects, all three languages allow the use of a class name as a type. Such types are not used to annotate objects, however, but to annotate variables, formal parameters, and formal result parameters. All three type systems are based on the idea that if, for example, a variable is annotated with the class name C, then the variable can contain instances of C or instances of subclasses of C.

We will use the term *class type* to describe the above use of a class name as a type. Given some notion of inheritance, a class type can be understood as a set of classes:

- a class type C denotes the set consisting of C and all possible subclasses of C.

This set can be illustrated as follows.

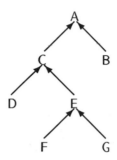

In the above hierarchy, the class type C corresponds to the infinite set {C,D,E,F,G,...}. We will call such a set a *cone* in the hierarchy of all possible classes. The idea behind this set interpretation of a class type is that if a variable is annotated with a class type C, then the variable can only contain instances of classes in the cone set for C.

The notion of class type does not depend on particular programs. The phrase "all possible subclasses of C" literally means all subclasses of C that it is possible to write. Thus, these classes need not be part of a particular program; they might be added later or perhaps not be added at all. The number of classes in a given program is of course *finite*, but the cone set of classes associated with a class type is infinite.

The typing rules for class types differ slightly between SIMULA, C++, and EIFFEL, as illustrated in the previous section. More details are given in the later chapter on type checking.

To simplify some of our later discussions of class types we now introduce a type syntax that resembles and simplifies the allowed type expressions in SIMULA, C++, and EIFFEL. The simplied syntax is as follows.

TYPE ::= Void | Int | Bool | ↑C

The meaning of the types is straightforward:

- the expression Void specifies a type that contains only the nil constant; it is patterned after the C type void;

- the expressions Int and Bool specify the sets of integer and boolean values, respectively; and
- the expression ↑C specifies a cone with root C, where C is a class name. The nil constant has any type ↑C.

The types Void, Int, and Bool are the basic part of the type system, and types of the form ↑C are the object-oriented part of the type system. Languages like EIFFEL that do not feature a nil can of course do without the Void type. In SIMULA, ↑C is written ref (C); in BETA, it is written ↑C; and in C++ and EIFFEL, it is simply written C.

This book generalizes the above type system. For example, the later chapter on type checking demonstrates how appropriate typing rules for the above type system can be derived from more general rules.

2.5   Why Something New?

Since so many object-oriented languages are perfectly happy with their existing type systems, then why are we proposing something new?

Our motive is not to promote yet another language. We want to explain general principles of object-oriented type systems and to propose insights and improvements that can be applied to all object-oriented languages. This is the basis for the design of our example language that will be presented in Chapter 3: it is intended to contain the common essence of the languages mentioned in the previous section. Our main contributions are the following.

- The class types may seem almost canonical, but they are simply instances of a more general system in which types are (finite or infinite) sets of classes. We present general type rules from which those for class types can be systematically derived. We also remedy various anomalies in existing systems and suggest practical extensions.
- There are no known type inference algorithms for languages with class types. Under the closed-world assumption we have developed successful algorithms for the more general set types, and we demonstrate how class types can be derived. Regardless of philosophy, this technique opens up for important optimizations during compilation. For untyped languages like SMALLTALK or SELF, the potential gain is even bigger than for typed ones.
- We discuss the many different variations of inheritance, and we present a new proposal that allows more of the essential superclass structure to be inherited by the subclass. We also present a novel well-formedness criterion for class hierarchies.
- We give a detailed discussion and comparison of SIMULA, C++, and EIFFEL's approaches to typing generic program parts, and we argue that none of them provide good solutions. Instead, we develop a new mechanism that fits well

together with inheritance; importantly, it works equally well for untyped languages.

In summary, we want to explain and improve existing type systems—not to overthrow them.

2.6 Why Not the λ-Calculus?

Apart from the practical work of language developers, there has been substantial theoretical work on type systems for object-like languages, mainly based on the λ-calculus. This section is directed towards the reader who is familiar with this approach and wants to relate it to ours.

Most type theories have been phrased for extensions of the λ-calculus. Originally, type theory was a discipline of logic, and only later did the relevance to programming emerge. Due to these origins, there is a gap between type theory and the types in commonly used languages. For example, the logician considers strong normalization an important result, but the programmer would seldomly want a type system that only accepted a subset of the terminating programs.

Lately, this gap has narrowed. The theorists have considered richer λ-calculi with elaborate constants and extra features that are inspired by developments in programming languages. The gap has even been bridged by languages like ML and MIRANDA, which have made a significant impression on both sides.

It makes good sense to use a common untyped language—the λ-calculus— as an experimental platform in the development of various type systems. The run-time model is stable and comparisons can be made on a formal basis. The disadvantage is that a fixed model may lead to misrepresentation of the concepts that are being investigated. For example, the λ-calculus does not directly support mutable variables and assignments, although they could be encoded, for example through the creation of modified copies. Depending on temperament, these situations are either worrying or the very process by which a deeper understanding is obtained.

Many important concepts have successfully been modeled in this manner, including higher-order functions, parametric polymorphism, recursive data types, abstract data types, and coercions.

For some time now, object-orientation has been a focal point of developments in programming languages, and the attentions of type theory have followed. The basic idea in the λ-calculus approach is to model an object as a record and a class as a record type. Instance variables are fields whose types are encodings of classes and methods are fields with function types.

With the "objects are records" perspective, it appeared to be natural to model inheritance by coercions. The subtype relation on records allows those with more fields to be smaller than those with fewer fields, since a coercion function can strip away the extra fields. Superficially, this corresponds well with subclasses having more fields and methods than superclasses. The idea turns out to be insufficient, however, when the run-time behavior is considered. The reason is that most object-oriented languages do not perform any coercions during parameter passing.

One improvement was the introduction of bounded universal quantification in the types of methods, thereby eliminating the need for coercion functions. This gave a closer match to the actual behavior of object-oriented languages. Still, however, no useful formal encoding of imperative updates has been given. Indeed, it has now been shown to be nearly impossible, since the required type only contains the identity function in a natural model. Furthermore, in some systems with bounded universal quantification, type checking has been shown to be undecidable.

One response to the update problem has been to disallow inheritance of mutable variables. This solves the problem by default but severely widens the gap to actual languages. Another approach has been to introduce records with both positive and negative information about fields. This can solve a narrow case of the update problem, but has not been worked out for a complete language. Moreover, the concept of negative fields is somewhat at odds with traditional object-oriented philosophy.

An entirely different problem relates to recursive classes. It turns out that encodings of recursive classes fail to obey the required subtype relationships. For purely functional languages, solutions have been presented using either F-bounded polymorphism or existential quantification.

A further problem concerns the contravariant ordering of function or method types. This is the natural choice for a coercion based theory and quite necessary for the traditional encodings. It is, however, somewhat controversial for object-oriented languages, even though there have been some attempts to justify it on purely methodological grounds. For a functional language with multi-methods, covariant method specialization has been encoded using sets of function types.

Finally, dynamic typing is never considered. Based on the logical tradition, a system that requires dynamic type checking is plain nonsense. This attitude should not be carried over to object-oriented languages, however, where dynamic type checks have been an integral part since the very beginnings.

In summary, the λ-calculus approach has made significant progress towards type systems for object-oriented languages, but no complete solution is in sight. The work has been interesting in its own right and has unveiled many novel language concepts. However, no significant impact on the type systems for existing object-oriented languages has been forthcoming. Our approach is to start with the run-time models of these languages and work from there.

Bibliographical Notes

This chapter has mentioned several object-oriented languages. The following table lists the developers and one or more references to introductory material on these languages.

Language	Developers	References
SIMULA	Dahl and Nygaard	[21, 20]
BETA	Kristensen, Madsen,	
	Møller-Pedersen, and Nygaard	[38]
SMALLTALK	Goldberg, Robson, and others	[26]
SELF	Ungar and Smith	[67, 1]
C++	Stroustrup	[63, 64]
OBJECTIVE-C	Cox	[19]
EIFFEL	Meyer	[45]

The name *class type* was first used by Meyer in connection with EIFFEL [45], although the underlying idea goes back to SIMULA.

The λ-calculus approach to object-oriented type systems was initiated by Cardelli in his seminal paper [10]. Cardelli and Wegner [12] introduced bounded universal quantification, and Bruce and Longo [7] proved that in a natural model of this system the type $\forall \sigma \leq \tau.\sigma \rightarrow \sigma$ contains only the identity function. The Cardelli/Wegner system was later streamlined by Cardelli, Mitchell, Martini, and Scedrov [9], and Pierce [58] proved that type checking in their system is undecidable. The introduction of F-bounded quantification in the Cardelli/Wegner system was suggested by Canning, Cook, Hill, Mitchell, and Olthoff [8]. The idea of positive and negative fields was proposed by Cardelli and Mitchell in [11]. Co-variant specialization of multi-methods was developed by Ghelli in [25].

There have been other approaches to object-oriented type systems, see the survey by Danforth and Tomlinson [22].

Exercises

1. Suppose that arbitrary integer values can be stored in variables. Suppose also that every subset of the integers is a valid type. Finally, suppose that we have a static type checker which accepts the assignment x:=y exactly when the type of x is a subset of the type of y. For example, the type checker accepts the following program.

    var p: $\{x \mid x \text{ is a prime} \wedge x > 2\}$
    var q: $\{x \mid x \text{ is odd}\}$
    q:=p

a) Explain how we can use this type checker to check the validity of formulas such as "7 is prime" and "2+2=4".

b) Goldbach's conjecture (yet neither proved nor falsified) states that every even number greater than 2 is the sum of two prime numbers. Use the type checker to decide this alleged theorem.

2. The table below will give an overview of the features found in various languages. Fill in each entry with a plus or a minus. The entries marked with ⋆ cannot be found in this chapter; try to find the information some other place.

	SIMULA	SMALLTALK	C++	EIFFEL
Classes				
Nested classes				⋆
Meta-classes		⋆		
Objects				
Inheritance				
Multiple inheritance	⋆	⋆	⋆	⋆
Method redefinition		⋆	⋆	⋆
Late binding				
Genericity	⋆	⋆	⋆	
Encapsulation		⋆	⋆	⋆
Super			⋆	⋆
Self	⋆		⋆	⋆
Inner		⋆	⋆	⋆
Type annotations				
Class types				
Static type checking				⋆
Dynamic type checking				⋆
Class inspection		⋆		⋆

3

The BOPL Language

This chapter introduces our basic object-oriented language; motivates its design; and presents its syntax and semantics along with some examples.

3.1 Motivation

The primary purpose of this book is to discuss the problems of appropriate type discipline for object-oriented languages and to present proposed solutions.

We reject an approach based on encodings into the λ-calculus because technical problems would force us to compromise the semantics of fundamental language mechanisms. However, the idea of having an untyped language model underlying our discussions is very appealing.

Accordingly, we shall define a simple object-oriented language which directly supports the essential features:

- classes and objects;
- assignments; and
- late binding.

Inheritance and genericity are not considered at this stage. These programming mechanisms will be introduced later and be realized through encodings into the more basic language. This is similar in spirit to the λ-approach; however, our target language includes more features directly.

The proposed language is called BOPL, which is an acronym for *Basic Object Programming Language*. It is mainly inspired by SMALLTALK, but the syntax has been made more PASCAL-like. It is our intention that the BOPL design should be entirely uncontroversial, containing the essential parts of such languages as SIMULA, SMALLTALK, C++, and EIFFEL. It is not our ambition to contribute to traditional language design issues concerning syntax, control structures, operators, or such.

The BOPL design is quite minimalistic; however, we claim that any missing parts are mostly irrelevant to typing issues or can be obtained as variations of those parts that are present. We deliberately include neither inheritance nor genericity, since we believe that most of the difficult typing problems are particular to the essential features mentioned above. The interplay between subclassing mechanisms and types will be studied separately in Chapters 6 and 7.

A BOPL program consists of a finite collection of *classes*, corresponding to the class library in SMALLTALK, followed by a main expression. As in SMALLTALK and C++, the evaluation of an expression yields a value and may modify the state.

A class defines named *instance variables* and *methods*. A method has a sequence of named *formal arguments* and a *body*, which is simply an expression.

An *object* is an instance of a particular class. When an object is created, it allocates room for the instance variables defined in its class. Each object contains explicit information about the class that it is an instance of. A *value* is either an integer, a boolean, a pointer to an object, or the constant nil.

Apart from trivial expressions and constants, we support *object creation*, *assignment* to instance variables, *conditionals*, *iteration*, *sequencing*, the self meta-variable, and *message sends* to objects, which must be interpreted by methods defined in their corresponding classes. Finally, we have the crucial ability to dynamically verify the class of an object.

In the following section we present the exact syntax; in Section 3.3 we make precise the run-time model that we are assuming; and in Section 3.4 we give an informal semantics of the various language constructs.

3.2   Syntax

Here is the context-free grammar for the language of BOPL programs. Non-terminals are written in THIS FONT and ε denotes the empty string.

```
PROGRAM          ::=  CLASSLIST? EXP

CLASSLIST?       ::=  ε | CLASSLIST
CLASSLIST        ::=  CLASS | CLASSLIST CLASS

CLASS            ::=  class ID VARLIST? METHODLIST? end |
                      class ID is ID

METHODLIST?      ::=  ε | METHODLIST
METHODLIST       ::=  METHOD | METHODLIST METHOD
METHOD           ::=  method ID FORMALS EXP end
```

VARLIST?	::=	ε | VARLIST
VARLIST	::=	VAR | VARLIST VAR
VAR	::=	**var** DEC
FORMALS	::=	(DECLIST?)
DECLIST?	::=	ε | DECLIST
DECLIST	::=	DEC | DECLIST ; DEC
DEC	::=	IDLIST
IDLIST	::=	ID | IDLIST , ID

EXP	::=	INT |
		EXP BINOP EXP |
		false |
		true |
		EXP **not** |
		ID := EXP |
		EXP ; EXP |
		if EXP **then** EXP **else** EXP **end** |
		while EXP **do** EXP **end** |
		nil |
		self |
		ID **new** |
		EXP **class new** |
		EXP **instance-of** { IDLIST } |
		ID |
		EXP . ID (EXPLIST?) |
		(EXP)
BINOP	::=	+ | − | * | = | **and** | **or** | <
EXPLIST?	::=	ε | EXPLIST
EXPLIST	::=	EXP | EXPLIST , EXP

INT	::=	DIGIT | DIGIT INT
DIGIT	::=	0 | 1 | 2 | 3 | 4 | 5 | 6 | 7 | 8 | 9
ID	::=	LETTER | ID LETTER | ID DIGIT
LETTER	::=	a | b | ... | z | A | B | ... | Z

3.3   Run-Time Model

A BOPL expression is evaluated in a *state* consisting of:

- the class library;
- the heap;

- the argument map; and
- the self object.

The *value* of an expression is either:

- the constant nil;
- an integer;
- a boolean; or
- a pointer to an object.

An *object* is a record that contains:

- the name of its class; and
- a value for each instance variable.

In this simple model we may view the *class library* as the textual representation of the classes declared in the program. The *heap* contains a collection of objects; all pointers refer to one of these objects. The *argument map* assigns values to the formal argument names of the surrounding method. The *self object* is the one that is currently active.

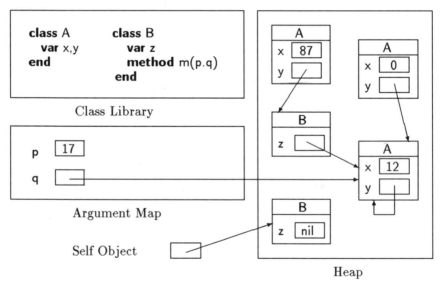

Heap

In the following section we explain the evaluation of expressions and how this modifies the state. The initial state for the main expression is of course a bit special, since it has neither a surrounding method nor an active object. Consequently, it consists of:

- the class library;
- an empty heap;

- an empty argument map; and
- an undefined self object.

A pictorial representation of a possible state is shown above.

3.4   Informal Semantics

We now present how each different kind of expression is evaluated. An expression always yields a value and its evaluation may change the state.

- Integer, boolean, and nil constants merely evaluate to their canonical values without changing the state.
- "EXP_1 BINOP EXP_2" first evaluates EXP_1 and then evaluates EXP_2 in the resulting state. The resulting value is finally obtained by performing the operator BINOP on the two intermediate values. For +, −, *, =, and <, both values must be integers; for and and or, both values must be booleans.
- "EXP not" first evaluates EXP; the resulting value must be a boolean, which is then negated.
- "ID := EXP" first evaluates EXP; in the resulting state, the instance variable named ID in the self object is then assigned the resulting value, which is also the resulting value of the assignment expression itself.
- "EXP_1 ; EXP_2" first evaluates EXP_1 and then evaluates EXP_2 in the resulting state. The resulting value is that of EXP_2.
- "**if** EXP_1 **then** EXP_2 **else** EXP_3 **end**" first evaluates EXP_1, which must yield a boolean value. If this value is **true**, then EXP_2 is evaluated; otherwise, EXP_3 is evaluated.
- "**while** EXP_1 **do** EXP_2 **end**" first evaluates EXP_1, which must yield a boolean value. If this value is **false**, then the resulting value is nil; otherwise, EXP_2 is evaluated and the **while**-loop is iterated.
- "self" does not change the state and evaluates to a pointer to the current self object.
- "ID **new**" looks up the class named ID in the class library and allocates a new object of that class, where all instance variables are initialized to nil. The resulting value is a pointer to the newly allocated object.
- "EXP **class new**" first evaluates EXP, which must yield a pointer to an object. Subsequently, a new object of the same class is created as described above.
- "EXP **instance-of** {IDLIST}" first evaluates EXP, which must yield a pointer to an object. If the class of that object is mentioned in IDLIST, then this object is the resulting value; otherwise, the result is a run-time error.
- "ID" first checks if the name is defined in the argument map. If so, then the result is the assigned value; otherwise, the search is extended to the instance variables of the self object.

This leaves only the message send "EXP . ID (EXPLIST?)" which is somewhat more complicated. Its evaluation is described in the following five points.

1) First EXP is evaluated. It must yield a pointer to an object r, called the *receiver*.
2) In the resulting state the expressions in EXPLIST? are evaluated from left to right while propagating the state. They yield the values $a_1, \ldots, a_n$ for some $n \geq 0$ and a final state f.
3) The class of the receiver is looked up in the class library, and in this class the implementation of a method named ID and accepting n arguments must be found. The implementation of the method will look like "**method** ID ($ID_1, \ldots, ID_n$) EXP_0 **end**".
4) Now, the expression EXP_0 is evaluated in a new state consisting of:

   — the class library of f;
   — the heap of f;
   — the argument map $[ID_1 \mapsto a_1, \ldots ID_n \mapsto a_n]$; and
   — the self object r.

   This results in a state c and a value v.
5) The resulting value is v and the resulting state consists of:

   — the class library of f;
   — the heap of c;
   — the argument map of f; and
   — the self object of f.

Implicit in steps 4) and 5) is the usual stack discipline of the dynamic chain of procedure calls.

Let us summarize the possibilities for run-time errors during the evaluation of expressions. Some are purely a matter of static scope rules, as follows. All referenced instance variables and formal arguments must be declared; definitions for all referenced class names must be present in the class library; and there can be no references to self in the main expression. We will assume that syntactically correct BOPL programs do not violate these requirements.

The genuine run-time errors, which we in the following shall be concerned with, are all occurrences of either:

• type mismatch in unary and binary operators;
• conditions in **if** and **while** not evaluating to booleans;
• the class of a receiver not implementing a method for the message it is being sent; or
• the receiver evaluating to nil.

Of these four errors, the last two ones, known as message-not-understood, are truly characteristic of object-oriented programming. In a purified version of e.g. SMALLTALK, the first two kinds of errors would also be special cases of message-not-understood.

In the following section we review the appropriateness of the BOPL design, and in Section 3.6 we provide some example programs.

3.5 What is Missing?

Clearly, BOPL falls short of being a realistic programming language. To some extent this is a deliberate choice, since we want a small, easily comprehensible language to study. This explains several omissions, such as:

- a full set of primitive values like floats, long integers, characters, etc.
- more varied control structures, such as **repeat**, **case**, or **loop**; and
- a proper interface including user input/output, a file system, and operating system access.

Such extensions would not contribute any novel typing problems, but would merely correspond to the introduction of more primitives.

Other restrictions seem less benign. Let us discuss some of the missing concepts that could raise concerns.

- *Privacy.* In BOPL classes, all methods can be accessed publicly. In contrast, many other languages present elaborate mechanisms for imposing restrictions. This is, however, more a question of access rules than of type rules.
- *Blocks.* In SMALLTALK, all control structures are programmed using blocks, which are expressions whose evaluations are suspended. Regarding types, a block can be viewed as a method in an anonymous class. The suspension of evaluation does not influence the type of the final result. In BOPL, we have restricted ourselves to a fixed collection of control structures.
- *Meta-classes.* In SMALLTALK, all classes are instances of meta-classes which describe their properties and for example implement the **new** methods for object creation. This model is not universally accepted and adds little to questions of typing. In BOPL, we have a primitive for **new**.
- *Nesting.* In many languages, class definitions can be nested in arbitrary levels. The BOPL language does not even allow local variables in methods. Again, this is a question of scope rules, since systematic renamings could represent a nested program correctly in our flat syntax.
- *Values.* In C++, values can be more than simply pointers to objects; records and arrays are also permitted. Since BOPL allows integers and booleans, we have already considered this in a modest form. Our approach to types could accommodate structured values, but at a cost in clarity and without much new insight about object-oriented programming.

- *Indexed variables.* SMALLTALK allows indexed variables that behave similarly to ordinary arrays. Again, their inclusion would not cause a problem for us, but we have chosen to omit them for simplicity. In examples, we use a version of arrays that is programmed in BOPL itself and is shown in Section 3.6.
- *Type-case.* EIFFEL allows the programmer to query the class of an object. Note that our **instance-of** cannot do this, since it generates a run-time error in the negative case. It would be simple enough to add such a construct, but we follow the principle that such control flow is better handled by late binding.

In general, we are willing to compromise full generality to focus more clearly on selected problems. We believe, however, that BOPL is sufficiently rich to make our results valid for realistic languages.

3.6   Examples

We show two useful data structures implemented in BOPL: *lists* and *arrays*. Linear lists are implemented in LISP-style by the following class.

```
class List
    var head, tail
    method Set(h, t)
        head := h;
        tail := t;
        self
    end
    method Cons(h)
        (self class new).Set(h, self)
    end
    method Car()
        head
    end
    method Cdr()
        tail
    end
end
```

```
(List new).Cons(13).Cons(12).Cons(11).Cdr().Car()
```

Here, the main expression evaluates to 12. Several details are noteworthy about the example.

The instance variables **head** and **tail** cannot be accessed directly, but only through the methods Set, Car and Cdr. The Set method is not really a part of the List interface and should be declared to be private—if that feature was supported in BOPL.

The use of **self class new** is in this case equivalent to List new. This construct relates to inheritance of recursive classes, which is discussed extensively in Chapter 6.

We use a well-known programming style in which methods that modify the object but do not compute a result always return the self object. This is the case for Set and Cons, and it allows cascaded sequences of message sends as the one displayed above.

To illustrate the run-time representation, we show in sequence below the contents of the heap before each of the five message sends. The receiver is in each case indicated by an incoming arrow without origin.

Initially, we compute the expression (List **new**). Its result, which is then the receiver of the message Cons(13), is:

The receiver of Cons(12) is:

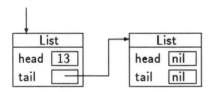

The receiver of Cons(11) is:

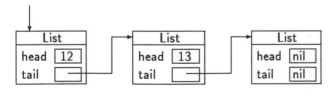

The receiver of Cdr( ) is:

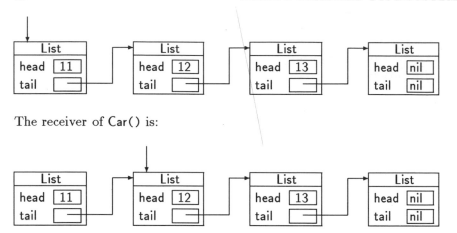

The receiver of Car() is:

which finally yields the result 12.

The following implementation of arrays will be used in future examples.

```
class Array
    var head, tail, length
    method at(i)
        if (i<0) or (length<i) then
            nil
        else
            if i = 0 then
                head
            else
                tail.at(i-1)
            end
        end
    end
    method atput(i, x)
        if (i<0) or (length<i) then
            self
        else
            if i = 0 then
                head := x
            else
                tail.atput(i-1, x)
            end
        end;
        self
    end
```

```
method initialize(size)
    if (size<0) or (size = 0) then
        self
    else
        tail := (Array new).initialize(size−1);
        length := size; self
    end
end
method arraysize()
    length
end
end
```

Bibliographical Notes

The BOPL language was created by extending the language studied by us in [55, 53]. The language in these two papers contains no integers and booleans and was designed with the purpose of being "as small as possible". That language resembles the O'SMALL language studied by Hense [31].

Object-oriented languages need not feature classes. Lieberman [40] and Borning [4] developed the notion of object-oriented languages based on prototypes. Wegner [71] suggested the terminology "object-based" for such languages.

Snyder [62] argued that instance variables should not be accessible by others than the object itself. Indeed, we have followed that advice in the BOPL design.

Exercises

1. Trace the execution of the following program by illustrating how the state changes.

    ```
    class Array
    ...
    end
    ```

    (Array new).initialize(5).atput(2, 87).atput(1, 14).at(2)

2. Consider the following extension of BOPL:

    METHOD ::=   method ID FORMALS VARLIST? EXP end

    The VARLIST? contains variables that are local to the method. Explain how such methods can be rewritten into BOPL. Be explicit about how you treat late binding and access to global variables. Apply your technique to each of the following two classes.

```
class X
    method m()
        var i
        i := 87
    end
end

class Y
    var g
    method n(p, q)
        var j
        self.n(j, g)
    end
end
```

3. Extend the class List from Section 3.6 with a method:

```
method append(x)
```

which appends the list x to the receiver.

4. Extend the class Array from Section 3.6 with a method:

```
method resize(size)
```

which changes the size of the receiver to size.

5. Write a class:

```
class Tree
    var val,left,right
    method Join(l, r)
    method Inc()
    method Sum()
end
```

whose objects represent binary trees with integer values in the nodes. The method Join combines two trees and returns a new root whose value is zero; Inc increments the value of the root of the receiver; and Sum returns the sum of the values of the nodes in the receiver.

6. Consider the following extension of BOPL:

```
EXP   ::=  [ EXP ]  |  EXP.value
```

The construct [EXP] is a block, that is, as suspended computation. A block is evaluated when it is sent the message **value**. Blocks can be assigned to variables, be passed as arguments, and be returned as results. A block can only refer to the variables and arguments that are visible at the place it is defined. Explain how blocks can be rewritten into plain BOPL. Apply your technique to each of the following two classes.

```
class X
   var i
   method m(a)
      i := i*i;
      [i+a]
   end
end

class Y
   var j
   method n(b)
      [j+[b].value]
   end
end
```

Consider then blocks with arguments as follows.

EXP   ::=   [VARLIST? **begin** EXP] | EXP.value (EXPLIST?)

If the number of formal and actual arguments do not match, then a run-time error occurs. Explain how blocks with arguments can be rewritten into plain BOPL. Apply your technique to the following program.

```
class Z
   var y
   method m(a)
      y := a*a;
      [z begin y+a+a]
   end
end

((Z new).m(7)).value(5)
```

What problems arise if blocks both can be nested and have arguments?

7. The blocks described in exercise 3.6 are traditionally used to implement
   control structures. Explain how the following class works and extend it
   with a similar method repeat.

```
class Do
   method while(b, e)
      if b.value then
         e.value; self.while(b, e)
      else
         nil
      end
   end
end
```

4

Type Checking

This chapter suggests that types should be sets of classes; presents a constraint-based approach to defining static type correctness of BOPL programs; shows how dynamic checks are inserted; and discusses the relationship to the class types used in existing languages.

4.1 Types are Sets of Classes

In Section 2.1 we concluded that type systems for programming languages must remedy three potential shortcomings of untyped languages by making them more readable, reliable, and efficient. These are in our opinion the primary goals, and we will present a type system that achieves that.

We shall develop the notion of types as *sets of classes*, which we claim is the canonical choice. It is not just another proposal, but rather a general model from which other type systems for object-oriented languages can be derived.

4.1.1 Types and Invariants

Types must specify invariants of the run-time behavior. Generally, variables and expressions are assigned types which classify values. The associated invariants are:

- that a variable can only contain values described by its type; and
- that an expression can only evaluate to values described by its type.

Note that neither classes nor methods will have individual types, since they are not values in most object-oriented languages.

We have four kinds of values in BOPL: integers, booleans, pointers to objects, and nil. The types must classify such values. We shall make one simplifying assumption, namely that a type must either include *all* integers or *none* of them, *both* booleans or *none* of them, and *all* pointers to objects of a specific class or *none* of them. Thus, for example, we are unable to specify a type of *even* integers.

Given this assumption, it seems rather obvious what types should be. A *token* is either Int, Bool, or the name of a class. A *type* is a set of tokens. Examples of types are:

- {}
- {Int}
- {Int, Bool, A, B, C}
- {Circle, Triangle, Rectangle}

The values classified by a type include the integers if Int belongs to the type, the booleans if Bool belongs to the type, and all pointers to objects of a class if its name belongs to the type. Furthermore, nil is always included, since it is the initial value of all variables.

We shall now observe how this concept of type satisfies our three requirements.

4.1.2 Readability

All explicit statements of invariants will in principle make programs easier to read and understand, in particular if they are integrated with an advanced browser in a programming environment. Thus, any kind of type annotation is potentially beneficial.

However, if the types themselves are obscure and hard to read, then little has been gained. The sets of classes are straightforward, since they only use notions already present in the programming language. No elaborate language of type expressions must be mastered.

Consider the following scenario with a hypothetical interactive browser for BOPL programs.

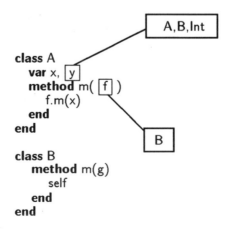

The "bubbles" are supposed to indicate the kind of information that can be obtained from either declared types—provided by the programmer—or inferred types—provided by the system. Thus, we can see that the instance variable y will only contain nil, integers, or pointers to objects of classes A or B. Also, the formal argument f will only contain nil or pointers to objects of class B.

4.1.3   Reliability

If a program annotated with sets of classes is known to be type correct, then it is easy to exclude certain run-time errors. Let us review the ones mentioned in Section 3.4.

- The type mismatch of binary operators can be ruled out. In the expression EXP_1 + EXP_2 we must simply ensure that the types of EXP_1 and EXP_2 are both {Int}.
- Conditions in **if** and **while** not evaluating to booleans can similarly be ruled out by ensuring that they have type {Bool}.
- The class of a receiver not implementing a method for the message it is being sent can be ruled out by ensuring that the type of the receiver exclusively contains classes that implement the given method.
- The nil receiver *cannot* always be detected because the receiver can be a never-terminating while loop.

Thus, if we can find a criterion for static type correctness, then we can eliminate most of the run-time errors in the BOPL language.

In the example above, we can see that the message send f.m(x) can never cause message-not-understood, since f can only be an object of class B which certainly implements a method for the message m.

4.1.4   Efficiency

Experiences from implementations of SMALLTALK and SELF show that information about the classes of possible receivers is the only real help to obtain run-time efficiency. Such information—which is contained in our types—allows inlining of methods, hashing of message sends, and removal of dead code. More abstract type systems may also ensure reliability, but none have been seen to significantly improve efficiency.

In the example above, a clever compiler can exploit the type information to avoid a dynamic dispatch for the message send f.m(x), by realizing that it is possible to inline the method from class B. Thus, it can instead generate code for the following, more efficient program.

```
class A
    var x, y
    method m(f)
        if f=nil then nil-receiver-error else f end
    end
end

class B
    method m(g)
        self
    end
end
```

This is of course not pure BOPL syntax, but rather a template for the code
that should be generated.

4.2   The Constraint Technique

This section presents a general technique for specifying static correctness,
which we shall make use of for the BOPL language.

In typed languages, such as PASCAL, type annotations are written various
places in programs. For example, variables and formal arguments will be
declared with types. From such places, types are propagated throughout the
program. Consider for example the following program.

```
var x,y: Integer;
var z: array [1..100] of Boolean;

writeln(x+y);
z[87] := true;
```

From the type declarations, it is immediate what are the types of x, y,
and z. However, the types of other variables and expressions must really be
inferred. For example, the type checker will decide that x+y has type Integer,
by consulting the types of x and y and the definition of +. Similarly, it is
inferred that z[87] is a variable of type Boolean.

A PASCAL manual will often contain long verbal descriptions of two different
parts of type checking:

- how to compute the types of all expressions and variables given the type
  declarations; and
- the constraints that these types must then satisfy.

We now present a more succinct and elegant constraint based technique.

In PASCAL, all variables and expressions have types but only some have explicit type declarations. However, it is possible to assign a type *variable* to every such entity. The values of some type variables are then known, whereas others must be inferred.

We shall use the notation $[\![E]\!]$ for the type variable denoting the type of E. The idea is now to define constraints on all these variables that simultaneously express:

- the declared type information;
- the propagation of types; and
- the requirements for static type correctness.

For the above PASCAL example, these constraints would look as follows.

$$[\![x]\!] = \mathsf{Integer}$$
$$[\![y]\!] = \mathsf{Integer}$$
$$[\![z]\!] = \mathbf{array}\ [1..100]\ \mathbf{of}\ \mathsf{Boolean}$$
$$[\![x]\!] = [\![y]\!]$$
$$[\![x]\!] = \mathsf{Integer} \Rightarrow [\![x{+}y]\!] = \mathsf{Integer}$$
$$[\![x]\!] = \mathsf{Real} \Rightarrow [\![x{+}y]\!] = \mathsf{Real}$$
$$[\![87]\!] = \mathsf{Integer}$$
$$[\![\mathsf{true}]\!] = \mathsf{Boolean}$$
$$[\![z\,[87]\,]\!] = [\![\mathsf{true}]\!]$$
$$[\![z]\!] = \mathbf{array}\ [1..100]\ \mathbf{of}\ [\![z\,[87]\,]\!]$$

The program is now seen to be statically type correct, because these constraints are solvable. Note how the overloading of + has been captured by conditional constraints.

The task of specifying static type correctness is that of showing how to systematically generate such constraints from the syntax. The task of checking static type correctness is that of deciding if the constraints are solvable.

Apart from gaining uniformity and succinctness, the advantage of this technique is the promise of a smooth transition from type checking to type inference. This aspect is explored further in Chapter 5.

4.3   Constraints for BOPL

We now present the type constraints for BOPL programs. This will take place in three steps. First, the syntax for type annotations must be given; second, the appropriate type variables must be defined; third, the constraints on these variables are presented.

4.3.1   Type Annotations

A program is typed when it contains type annotations. Our types are sets of classes; hence, if they are finite, then they can be written as simply sequences of class names. For now we will allow only finite sets; class types will be considered in Section 4.6. We will attach types three places in programs:

- at instance variables; the associated invariant is that the instance variable can only contain nil or the values described by the type;
- at formal arguments; the associated invariant is the same as for instance variables; and
- at method results; the associated invariant is that the body of the method can only evaluate to values described by the type.

The language of typed programs modifies the BOPL syntax as follows.

METHOD	::=	**method** ID FORMALS **returns** TYPE EXP **end**
DEC	::=	IDLIST : TYPE
TYPE	::=	TOKEN | {TOKENLIST?}
TOKENLIST?	::=	ε | TOKENLIST
TOKENLIST	::=	TOKEN | TOKENLIST TOKEN
TOKEN	::=	Int | Bool | ID

Note that singleton sets can be written without enclosing braces. The following is an example of an annotated program.

```
class A
    var x: A
    var y: {A,B,Int}
    method m(f: B) returns B
        f.m(x)
    end
end

class B
    method m(g: A) returns B
        self
    end
end

(A new).m(B new).m(nil)
```

Some examples of the invariants stated by these annotations are:

- the instance variable y can only contain nil, integers, or pointers to objects of classes A or B;
- the method m in class A will always return either nil or a pointer to an object of class B; and
- the formal argument g of method m in class B will only accept nil or a pointer to an object of class A.

As mentioned several times, it is formally undecidable whether such invariants are valid. Thus, we must develop a criterion for *static* type correctness that conservatively approximates type correctness. We shall use the technique of type variables and constraints. The static type analysis of the above example program is detailed in Section 4.3.4.

4.3.2   Type Variables

In essence, we will assign a type variable to every expression, instance variable, and formal argument. A minor syntactic convention will allow us to name these variables in a particularly intuitive manner.

Henceforth, we shall assume that in every program all instance variables and formal arguments have distinct names. This could of course easily be obtained through generous renaming without changing the semantics. With this in mind, we can use the notation:

$$[\![x]\!], \ [\![f]\!], \ \text{and} \ [\![E]\!]$$

for the type variables associated with the instance variable x, the formal argument f, and the expression E. Notice that two different occurrences of syntactically identical expressions will be assigned the same type variable. This is a sound simplification, since the expressions will also have identical types due to our naming convention.

We need, however, to distinguish between the type variables associated with the self meta-variables for the different classes. Thus, for the class C we shall use the notation $[\![\text{self-C}]\!]$.

4.3.3   Type Constraints

The required type constraints are specified inductively in the grammar of the BOPL language. Thus each kind of expression will contribute its own particular constraints.

The following is a systematic description of these different constraints. In each case we will argue that the semantics is soundly reflected.

1)   "INT". For any integer constant k we have the constraint:

$$[\![k]\!] = \{\text{Int}\}$$

This states that an integer constant evaluates to an integer value.

2) "true" and "false". For the boolean constants we have the constraints:

$$[\![\text{true}]\!] = \{\text{Bool}\} \quad \text{and} \quad [\![\text{false}]\!] = \{\text{Bool}\}$$

This states that both the boolean constants evaluate to boolean values.

3) "nil". For the nil constant we have the constraint:

$$[\![\text{nil}]\!] = \{\}$$

This is sound, since nil evaluates to neither an integer value, a boolean value, nor a pointer to an object.

4) "EXP_1 + EXP_2". For the addition, the constraints are:

$$[\![\text{EXP}_1]\!] = \{\text{Int}\}$$
$$[\![\text{EXP}_2]\!] = \{\text{Int}\}$$
$$[\![\text{EXP}_1 + \text{EXP}_2]\!] = \{\text{Int}\}$$

This states that the arguments must be integer values and that the result will be an integer value.

5) "EXP_1 - EXP_2". For the subtraction, the constraints are:

$$[\![\text{EXP}_1]\!] = \{\text{Int}\}$$
$$[\![\text{EXP}_2]\!] = \{\text{Int}\}$$
$$[\![\text{EXP}_1 - \text{EXP}_2]\!] = \{\text{Int}\}$$

This states that the arguments must be integer values and that the result will be an integer value.

6) "EXP_1 * EXP_2". For the multiplication, the constraints are:

$$[\![\text{EXP}_1]\!] = \{\text{Int}\}$$
$$[\![\text{EXP}_2]\!] = \{\text{Int}\}$$
$$[\![\text{EXP}_1 * \text{EXP}_2]\!] = \{\text{Int}\}$$

This states that the arguments must be integer values and that the result will be an integer value.

7) "EXP_1 = EXP_2". For the equality, the constraints are:

$$[\![\text{EXP}_1]\!] = \{\text{Int}\}$$
$$[\![\text{EXP}_2]\!] = \{\text{Int}\}$$
$$[\![\text{EXP}_1 = \text{EXP}_2]\!] = \{\text{Bool}\}$$

This states that the arguments must be integer values and that the result will be a boolean value.

8) "EXP_1 and EXP_2". For the conjunction, the constraints are:

$$[\![\text{EXP}_1]\!] = \{\text{Bool}\}$$
$$[\![\text{EXP}_2]\!] = \{\text{Bool}\}$$
$$[\![\text{EXP}_1 \text{ and } \text{EXP}_2]\!] = \{\text{Bool}\}$$

This states that the arguments must be boolean values and that the result will be a boolean value.

9) "EXP_1 or EXP_2". For the disjunction, the constraints are:

$$[\![\text{EXP}_1]\!] = \{\text{Bool}\}$$
$$[\![\text{EXP}_2]\!] = \{\text{Bool}\}$$
$$[\![\text{EXP}_1 \text{ or } \text{EXP}_2]\!] = \{\text{Bool}\}$$

This states that the arguments must be boolean values and that the result will be a boolean value.

10) "$\text{EXP}_1 < \text{EXP}_2$". For the inequality, the constraints are:

$$[\![\text{EXP}_1]\!] = \{\text{Int}\}$$
$$[\![\text{EXP}_2]\!] = \{\text{Int}\}$$
$$[\![\text{EXP}_1 < \text{EXP}_2]\!] = \{\text{Bool}\}$$

This states that the arguments must be integer values and that the result will be an integer value.

11) "EXP not". For the negation, the constraints are:

$$[\![\text{EXP}]\!] = \{\text{Bool}\}$$
$$[\![\text{EXP} \text{ not}]\!] = \{\text{Bool}\}$$

This states that the argument must be a boolean value and that the result will be a boolean value.

12) "$\text{ID} := \text{EXP}$". For the assignment, the constraints are:

$$[\![\text{EXP}]\!] \subseteq [\![\text{ID}]\!]$$
$$[\![\text{ID} := \text{EXP}]\!] = [\![\text{EXP}]\!]$$

The first constraint states that any resulting value of EXP is a possible value of the instance variable ID. We cannot have an equality here, since other assignments may also contribute to ID. The other constraint states that the resulting value of the assignment is that of EXP.

13) "EXP_1 ; EXP_2". For the sequence, the constraint is:

$$[\![\text{EXP}_1 \text{ ; } \text{EXP}_2]\!] = [\![\text{EXP}_2]\!]$$

This states that the resulting value of a sequence is that of the second expression EXP_2.

14) "**if** EXP$_1$ **then** EXP$_2$ **else** EXP$_3$ **end**". For the conditional, the constraints are:

$$\llbracket \text{EXP}_1 \rrbracket = \{\text{Bool}\}$$
$$\llbracket \textbf{if } \text{EXP}_1 \textbf{ then } \text{EXP}_2 \textbf{ else } \text{EXP}_3 \textbf{ end} \rrbracket = \llbracket \text{EXP}_2 \rrbracket \cup \llbracket \text{EXP}_3 \rrbracket$$

The first constraint states that the condition EXP$_1$ must evaluate to a boolean value. The other constraint states that the resulting value is that of either EXP$_2$ or EXP$_3$. Here we see an example of the inherent imprecision of static type correctness: it must pessimistically consider both branches of the conditional expression. A complete knowledge of the run-time behavior might allow one of the branches to be ruled out.

15) "**while** EXP$_1$ **do** EXP$_2$ **end**". For the iteration, the constraints are:

$$\llbracket \text{EXP}_1 \rrbracket = \{\text{Bool}\}$$
$$\llbracket \textbf{while } \text{EXP}_1 \textbf{ do } \text{EXP}_2 \textbf{ end} \rrbracket = \{\}$$

The first constraint states that the condition EXP$_1$ must evaluate to a boolean value. The other constraint reflects that the resulting value of a **while**-expression is nil.

16) "**self**". The constraint for the **self** meta-variable is:

$$\llbracket \text{self-C} \rrbracket = \{\text{C}\}$$

where C is the statically enclosing class. This reflects that **self** evaluates to a pointer to an object of the class in which the expression occurs. This depends of course on the particular program that surrounds this expression.

17) "ID **new**". The constraint for object creation is:

$$\llbracket \text{ID } \textbf{new} \rrbracket = \{\text{ID}\}$$

This states that the expression evaluates to a pointer to an object of the given class.

18) "EXP **class new**". The constraints for the indirect object creation are:

$$\llbracket \text{EXP} \rrbracket \subseteq \{ \textit{all classes} \}$$
$$\llbracket \text{EXP } \textbf{class new} \rrbracket = \llbracket \text{EXP} \rrbracket$$

This first constraint states that EXP must evaluate to a pointer to an object, i.e., it may not evaluate to either an integer or a boolean value. Again, this depends on the surrounding program. The other constraint reflects that the expression evaluates to a pointer to an object of the same class as that of EXP.

19) "EXP **instance-of** {IDLIST}". The constraint for the dynamic check of class membership is:

$$[\![\text{EXP } \textbf{instance-of } \{ \text{ IDLIST } \}]\!] = \{ \text{ IDLIST } \}$$

This states that the expression can only successfully evaluate to a pointer to an object of one of the classes mentioned in IDLIST. Of course, the potential run-time error is not mentioned in the static type correctness; the validity of the corresponding invariant is simply assumed. This shows how static and dynamic type checks interact.

20) "ID". For a variable or a formal argument, we have the constraint:

$$[\![\text{ID}]\!] = \textit{the declared type}$$

The phrasing of this constraint is once again dependent on the rest of the program.

This leaves only the message send "EXP . ID (EXP_1, ..., EXP_n)" for which the constraints are less obvious. We shall present them in several steps below.

First of all, EXP must evaluate to a pointer to an object. In order to ensure that the receiver will understand the message ID, we must further require that all receiver objects are of classes that implement a method named ID accepting n arguments. Thus, we have the constraint:

21)
$$[\![\text{EXP}]\!] \subseteq \{ \textit{all legal receiver classes} \}$$

where legality is as described above. For a given program, this expands to an actual set of classes. Now, consider a legal receiver class C, which implements the method

> **method** ID (ID_1: TYPE_1, ..., ID_n: TYPE_n) **returns** TYPE
> EXP_0
> **end**

We define *conditional* constraints that reflect the effect of a potential message send. They look like:

22)

$$C \in [\![\text{EXP}]\!] \Rightarrow \begin{cases} [\![\text{EXP}_1]\!] \subseteq [\![\text{ID}_1]\!] \\ \quad\vdots \\ [\![\text{EXP}_n]\!] \subseteq [\![\text{ID}_n]\!] \\ [\![\text{EXP . ID (EXP}_1, ..., \text{EXP}_n)]\!] \supseteq \text{TYPE} \supseteq [\![\text{EXP}_0]\!] \end{cases}$$

The first n constraints reflect that the values of the actual arguments are assigned to the formal arguments. The final constraint reflects that the value of the body of the method becomes the result of the message send and must conform to the declared result type.

In summary, constraints are generated systematically from the syntax of programs. For certain expressions, it is necessary to consider the surrounding program in order to phrase the constraints. Given that a set equality can be rephrased as two set inclusions, it is seen that all type constraints uniformly appear to be conditional set inclusions between type variables or constants.

A BOPL program is defined to be statically type correct if the constraints generated from its syntax are solvable.

4.3.4   Examples

Consider the small nonsense program introduced in Section 4.3.1. For future reference, we enumerate its lines.

```
1    class A
2        var x: A
3        var y: {A,B,Int}
4        method m(f: B) returns B
5            f.m(x)
6        end
7    end
8
9    class B
10       method m(g: A) returns B
11           self
12       end
13   end
14
15   (A new).m(B new).m(nil)
```

Below is the full collection of constraints defining its static correctness. For each constraint, we have indicated its origin using the above enumeration of the program lines *(italics)* and the general constraints (roman).

2)	20)	$[\![x]\!] = \{A\}$
3)	20)	$[\![y]\!] = \{A,B,Int\}$
4)	20)	$[\![f]\!] = \{B\}$
10)	20)	$[\![g]\!] = \{A\}$
5)	21)	$[\![f]\!] \subseteq \{A,B\}$
5)	22)	$A \in [\![f]\!] \Rightarrow \begin{cases} [\![x]\!] \subseteq [\![f]\!] \\ [\![f.m(x)]\!] \supseteq \{B\} \supseteq [\![f.m(x)]\!] \end{cases}$

$5)$ $22)$ $B \in \llbracket f \rrbracket \Rightarrow \begin{cases} \llbracket x \rrbracket \subseteq \llbracket g \rrbracket \\ \llbracket f.m(x) \rrbracket \supseteq \{B\} \supseteq \llbracket self\text{-}B \rrbracket \end{cases}$

$11)$ $16)$ $\llbracket self\text{-}B \rrbracket = \{B\}$

$15)$ $17)$ $\llbracket A \ \mathbf{new} \rrbracket = \{A\}$

$15)$ $17)$ $\llbracket B \ \mathbf{new} \rrbracket = \{B\}$

$15)$ $21)$ $\llbracket A \ \mathbf{new} \rrbracket \subseteq \{A,B\}$

$15)$ $22)$ $A \in \llbracket A \ \mathbf{new} \rrbracket \Rightarrow \begin{cases} \llbracket B \ \mathbf{new} \rrbracket \subseteq \llbracket f \rrbracket \\ \llbracket (A \ \mathbf{new}).m(B \ \mathbf{new}) \rrbracket \supseteq \{B\} \supseteq \llbracket f.m(x) \rrbracket \end{cases}$

$15)$ $22)$ $B \in \llbracket A \ \mathbf{new} \rrbracket \Rightarrow \begin{cases} \llbracket B \ \mathbf{new} \rrbracket \subseteq \llbracket g \rrbracket \\ \llbracket (A \ \mathbf{new}).m(B \ \mathbf{new}) \rrbracket \supseteq \{B\} \supseteq \llbracket self\text{-}B \rrbracket \end{cases}$

$15)$ $3)$ $\llbracket nil \rrbracket = \{\}$

$15)$ $21)$ $\llbracket (A \ \mathbf{new}).m(B \ \mathbf{new}) \rrbracket \subseteq \{A,B\}$

$15)$ $22)$ $A \in \llbracket (A \ \mathbf{new}).m(B \ \mathbf{new}) \rrbracket \Rightarrow$
$\begin{cases} \llbracket nil \rrbracket \subseteq \llbracket f \rrbracket \\ \llbracket (A \ \mathbf{new}).m(B \ \mathbf{new}).m(nil) \rrbracket \supseteq \{B\} \supseteq \llbracket f.m(x) \rrbracket \end{cases}$

$15)$ $22)$ $B \in \llbracket (A \ \mathbf{new}).m(B \ \mathbf{new}) \rrbracket \Rightarrow$
$\begin{cases} \llbracket nil \rrbracket \subseteq \llbracket g \rrbracket \\ \llbracket (A \ \mathbf{new}).m(B \ \mathbf{new}).m(nil) \rrbracket \supseteq \{B\} \supseteq \llbracket self\text{-}B \rrbracket \end{cases}$

It does in fact admit a solution; hence, the program is deemed statically correct, and it is guaranteed not to cause certain run-time errors. The solution is as follows.

$$\llbracket x \rrbracket = \{A\}$$
$$\llbracket y \rrbracket = \{A,B,Int\}$$
$$\llbracket f \rrbracket = \{B\}$$
$$\llbracket g \rrbracket = \{A\}$$
$$\llbracket f.m(x) \rrbracket = \{B\}$$
$$\llbracket self\text{-}B \rrbracket = \{B\}$$
$$\llbracket A \ \mathbf{new} \rrbracket = \{A\}$$
$$\llbracket B \ \mathbf{new} \rrbracket = \{B\}$$
$$\llbracket (A \ \mathbf{new}).m(B \ \mathbf{new}) \rrbracket = \{B\}$$
$$\llbracket nil \rrbracket = \{\}$$
$$\llbracket (A \ \mathbf{new}).m(B \ \mathbf{new}).m(nil) \rrbracket = \{B\}$$

In contrast, the following program is not statically correct.

```
1    class C
2        method n(i: Int) returns Int
3            i+1
4        end
5    end
6
7    (C new).n(true)
```

Its constraints are given below.

2,3)	4), 20)	$[\![i]\!] = \{\mathsf{Int}\}$
3)	1), 4)	$[\![1]\!] = \{\mathsf{Int}\}$
3)	4)	$[\![i + 1]\!] = \{\mathsf{Int}\}$
7)	17)	$[\![C\ \mathbf{new}]\!] = \{C\}$
7)	2)	$[\![\mathsf{true}]\!] = \{\mathsf{Bool}\}$
7)	21)	$[\![C\ \mathbf{new}]\!] \subseteq \{C\}$
7)	22)	$C \in [\![C\ \mathbf{new}]\!] \Rightarrow \left\{ \begin{array}{l} [\![\mathsf{true}]\!] \subseteq [\![i]\!] \\ [\![(C\ \mathbf{new}).\mathsf{n}(\mathsf{true})]\!] \supseteq \{\mathsf{Int}\} \supseteq [\![i + 1]\!] \end{array} \right.$

They admit no solution, since they imply:

$$\{\mathsf{Bool}\} = [\![\mathsf{true}]\!] \subseteq [\![i]\!] = \{\mathsf{Int}\}$$

This is satisfactory, since the program would clearly cause a run-time error. Finally, consider this trivial program.

$$(\mathbf{if}\ \mathsf{true}\ \mathbf{then}\ 0\ \mathbf{else}\ \mathsf{false}\ \mathbf{end}) + 1$$

Its constraints are the following.

1)	$[\![0]\!] = \{\mathsf{Int}\}$
1), 4)	$[\![1]\!] = \{\mathsf{Int}\}$
2), 14)	$[\![\mathsf{false}]\!] = \{\mathsf{Bool}\}$
14)	$[\![\mathbf{if}\ \mathsf{true}\ \mathbf{then}\ 0\ \mathbf{else}\ \mathsf{false}\ \mathbf{end}]\!] = [\![0]\!] \cup [\![\mathsf{false}]\!]$
4)	$[\![\mathbf{if}\ \mathsf{true}\ \mathbf{then}\ 0\ \mathbf{else}\ \mathsf{false}\ \mathbf{end}]\!] = \{\mathsf{Int}\}$
4)	$[\![(\mathbf{if}\ \mathsf{true}\ \mathbf{then}\ 0\ \mathbf{else}\ \mathsf{false}\ \mathbf{end}) + 1]\!] = \{\mathsf{Int}\}$

They are unsolvable, since they imply:

$$\{\mathsf{Bool}\} = [\![\mathsf{false}]\!] \subseteq [\![\mathbf{if}\ \mathsf{true}\ \mathbf{then}\ 0\ \mathbf{else}\ \mathsf{false}\ \mathbf{end}]\!] = \{\mathsf{Int}\}$$

Hence, the program is statically incorrect and will be rejected by the compiler. However, the program will run without errors, so in this case the requirements are stricter than necessary. As indicated earlier, for any sound and decidable definition of static correctness, there must be cases similar to this one.

4.4   The Type Checking Algorithm

In the previous examples, it was fairly easy both to generate the constraints and to determine if they were solvable. But, in general, programs will be much larger and the corresponding constraints may be less obvious. Then how do we determine solvability and, hence, static correctness?

It turns out to be straightforward, since the types of all expressions depend functionally on the declared types. If we had a more polymorphic syntax, then the task could be much more difficult.

The static type checking algorithm works by performing a recursive traversal of the syntax trees, while maintaining two *type environments*:

- the *global* environment contains a complete description of all classes and methods. Thus, one can inspect the types of all instance variables, formal arguments, and method results; and
- the *local* environment contains the name of the statically enclosing class as well as the names and types of the surrounding instance variables and formal arguments.

Given two such environments, which are easily maintained during a traversal of the class library, any expression can be type checked. We have a function $\text{TC}(\mathcal{G},\mathcal{L},\text{EXP})$ which type checks the expression EXP—relatively to the global environment $\mathcal{G}$ and the local environment $\mathcal{L}$—and simultaneously computes its type. The TC function is defined inductively in the grammar. We show a few illustrative cases. For equality of integers we have:

$\text{TC}(\mathcal{G},\mathcal{L},\text{EXP}_1 = \text{EXP}_2) =$
    if $\text{TC}(\mathcal{G},\mathcal{L},\text{EXP}_1) = \{\text{Int}\} \wedge \text{TC}(\mathcal{G},\mathcal{L},\text{EXP}_2) = \{\text{Int}\}$ **then**
       $\{\text{Bool}\}$
    else
       type error
    end

This is a simple recursive traversal. We use the notation *type error* to indicate a global exception that terminates the computation. For the assignment we have:

$\text{TC}(\mathcal{G},\mathcal{L},\text{ID} := \text{EXP}) =$
    let te $= \text{TC}(\mathcal{G},\mathcal{L},\text{EXP})$ **in**
    if te $\subseteq \mathcal{L}(\text{ID})$ **then**
       te
    else
       type error
    end

For the conditional we have:

$\text{TC}(\mathcal{G},\mathcal{L},$ **if** EXP_1 **then** EXP_2 **else** EXP_3 **end**$) =$
    let $\text{te}_1 = \text{TC}(\mathcal{G},\mathcal{L},\text{EXP}_1)$ **in**
    let $\text{te}_2 = \text{TC}(\mathcal{G},\mathcal{L},\text{EXP}_2)$ **in**
    let $\text{te}_3 = \text{TC}(\mathcal{G},\mathcal{L},\text{EXP}_3)$ **in**
    if $\text{te}_1 = \{\text{Bool}\}$ **then**

$$\text{te}_2 \cup \text{te}_3$$
else
> *type error*

end

For the message send we have:

$$\text{TC}(\mathcal{G},\mathcal{L},\text{EXP}.\text{ID}(\text{EXP}_1, \ldots, \text{EXP}_n)) =$$
let $\text{te} = \text{TC}(\mathcal{G},\mathcal{L},\text{EXP})$ **in**
let $\text{te}_1 = \text{TC}(\mathcal{G},\mathcal{L},\text{EXP}_1)$ **in**

$\vdots$

let $\text{te}_n = \text{TC}(\mathcal{G},\mathcal{L},\text{EXP}_n)$ **in**
if $\text{te} = \{\}$ **then** *no receivers* **else**
> $\bigcup_{C \, \in \, \text{te}} \text{TC-CLASS}(\mathcal{G},\text{C})$

end

The error *no receivers* indicates that the receiver expression will evaluate to nil or loop infinitely; hence, the message can never be successful. For each possible receiver class, the following TC-CLASS function evaluates to the result type.

$$\text{TC-CLASS}(\mathcal{G},\text{C}) =$$
if $\mathcal{G}(\text{C})$ *contains the method implementation*
> "**method** $\text{ID}(\text{ID}_1:\text{TYPE}_1, \ldots, \text{ID}_n:\text{TYPE}_n)$ **returns** TYPE"

then
> **if** $\forall i$: $\text{te}_i \subseteq \text{TYPE}_i$ **then**
> > TYPE
>
> **else**
> > *type error*
>
> **end**

else
> *message not understood*

end

The error *message not understood* indicates that at least one potential receiver does not implement an appropriate method.

The remaining cases are easily obtained as variations of the above. The type of every expression can be computed from the types of its subexpressions. Thus, type checking can be implemented efficiently. In Chapter 5, we shall see that type inference is more of an algorithmic challenge.

4.5   Dynamic Type Checks

Dynamic type checks are necessary in object-oriented languages. We motivate
this with an example and discuss how it influences the type checker.

4.5.1   Motivation

The late binding of messages allows a code fragment to make sense when
applied to objects of several different classes. For example, if we have three
classes Circle, Rectangle, and Triangle that each implement the methods
Translate and Print, then this fragment is sensible regardless of the particular
class of g:

> g.Translate(100,200);
> g.Print

Our type system reflects these possibilities by allowing variables to contain
objects of several different classes. Thus, we could define a class Application
with a method:

> **method** TransPrint(g: {Circle,Rectangle,Triangle})
> > > > **returns** {Circle,Rectangle,Triangle}
> > g.Translate(100,200);
> > g.Print;
> > g
> **end**

which accepts as argument an object of any of the three geometric classes,
which is then translated, printed, and returned. Small examples may
sometimes seem contrived, but hopefully it is clear that this situation occurs
often and in many guises in object-oriented programming. Other typical
examples arise from applications of container classes, such as lists and arrays.

Suppose now that c is a variable of type Circle. A reasonable expression
would seem to be:

> c := (Application **new**).TransPrint(c)

but this is of course rejected by the type checker, since the result type of the
method is larger than the type of c.

This is somewhat unsatisfactory, since the programmer *knows* that the
returned value is an object of class Circle. In an untyped language anything
goes—including the successful execution of such expressions. Typed languages
have basically three possible responses to this problem:

- the program has been rejected for a good reason,
    The compiler responds: "I know what I am doing. Go away!";

- the programmer may explicitly insert a dynamic check,
   The compiler responds: "This is not my problem, its yours!"; or
- the compiler will implicitly insert a dynamic check;
   The compiler responds: "I will take care of this!".

The first two options require nothing extra of the compiler. The last option is more challenging and we will in the following demonstrate what the compiler can do in this case. In the above example, the expression would be transformed into:

$$c := ((\text{Application } \textbf{new}).\text{TransPrint}(c) \textbf{ instance-of } \text{Circle})$$

Now the assignment will type check, since the right-hand expression is guaranteed to evaluate to a Circle object; otherwise, a run-time error would occur.

4.5.2   How to Insert Dynamic Checks

What are the general rules for inserting such dynamic checks? As with all actions based on inferred information, a delicate balancing act is required. If dynamic checks are inserted blindly, then any program will be accepted by the compiler, as if it was untyped. However, we still want to make use of the declared type information as far as possible. An appropriate strategy is the following, where the options must be considered in the order of presentation.

1) When a program fragment is statically correct, then it is accepted and no dynamic checks are inserted.
2) When a program fragment is statically incorrect but might succeed at run-time, then it is accepted and dynamic checks are inserted.
3) When a program fragment is statically incorrect and cannot succeed at run-time, then it is rejected.

In this manner, we minimize the number of dynamic checks and filter out most meaningless programs.

Dynamic checks can be inserted in connection with assignments, argument passings, and values returned from method invocations. All three may be understood as a kind of assignment. In each case, a set inclusion is required to hold between two types. For the assignment ID := EXP the constraint is:

$$[\![\text{ID}]\!] \supseteq [\![\text{EXP}]\!]$$

The three cases in our strategy can be recognized as follows.

1) $[\![\text{ID}]\!] \supseteq [\![\text{EXP}]\!]$. The expression will always evaluate to an object of a legal class.

2) $[\![\text{ID}]\!] \cap [\![\text{EXP}]\!] \neq \{\}$. The expression might evaluate to an object of a legal class. The program is accepted after the assignment has been transformed into ID := (EXP **instance-of** $[\![\text{ID}]\!]$).

3) $[\![\text{ID}]\!] \cap [\![\text{EXP}]\!] = \{\}$. The expression cannot possibly evaluate to an object of a legal class. The program is rejected.

This is almost the full story. There are only a few modifications for the cases with arguments and return values. For an argument passing, the right-hand set is the type of the actual argument, whereas the left-hand set is the *intersection* of the corresponding formal argument types from all the possible receivers. For a return value, the right-hand set is the type of the method body, and the left-hand set is the declared result type.

The idea of compiler-directed dynamic checks was first introduced in SIMULA. It has many advantages over the dynamic check performed during method lookup in untyped languages such as SMALLTALK. First, much fewer checks are required, since the declared type information is also employed. Second, run-time errors will generally be caught earlier during the computation, thus preventing error propagation that can make debugging more difficult.

In our model, type checking becomes a program transformation, since dynamic checks may be inserted into the program text. Consider for example the following classes.

```
class A
    var x: {Int, Bool}
    var y: Int
    method m(f: A) returns Int
        y := x
    end
end

class B
    method m(g: {A, B}) returns Int
        g.m(g)
    end
end
```

They are not statically correct, and the type checker will transform them as follows.

```
class A
    var x: {Int, Bool}
    var y: Int
```

```
        method m(f: A) returns Int
            y :=  (x instance-of Int)
        end
    end

    class B
        method m(g: {A, B}) returns Int
            g.m( g instance-of A )
        end
    end
```

The program is now statically correct. Type checking is *idempotent*: two applications will yield the same result as just one. The following program was in Section 4.3.4 seen to be statically incorrect.

```
    class C
        method n(i: Int) returns Int
            i+1
        end
    end
```

    (C new).n(true)

The type checker will not insert dynamic checks. Instead, the program is rejected because of the observation that:

$$[\![\text{true}]\!] \cap [\![\text{i}]\!] = \{\text{Bool}\} \cap \{\text{Int}\} = \{\}$$

which means that the argument passing cannot possibly succeed at run-time.

4.6   Class Types

This section demonstrates how typing rules for class types can be derived from the more general rules in this chapter. It also briefly compares them with the typing rules of SIMULA, C++, and EIFFEL.

4.6.1   Infinite Sets

So far, we have assumed that types are *finite* sets of classes. This has been emphasized by the BOPL type syntax which allows only a listing of the elements. We could have chosen other, more indirect, ways of specifying types. For example, consider the following declaration.

    var x: [Init, Push, Pop]

This syntax specifies the set of all classes that implement methods named Init, Push, and Pop. For any given program, only finitely many classes will have this property. Thus, under the closed-world assumption, the above syntax is a convenient shorthand for a finite set. Note that we do not have to define new type rules for this syntax. It is sufficient to expand it into a finite set and then apply the already established rules.

Our type rules are sound not only for finite sets but also for *infinite* sets. This means that we can adopt the open-world assumption and interpret for example class types or the above type syntax as infinite sets. The open-world assumption yields an infinite set from for example a class type because the type expression is notionally expanded with respect to *all* classes—not just the ones that occur in the given program. This enables separate compilation; when a new class is written, the types stay the same. In contrast, when expanding types under the closed-world assumption, the types may change when a new class is written. Such changes of course require new type checking of all classes.

The open-world assumption—and thus infinite sets—yields a challenge for the type checker: can the type constraints be verified? This question is not of concern when using the closed-world assumption, because then the sets are finite. But with the open-world assumption it might with an unwise choice of type expressions be impossible to decide, for example, if one set is a subset of another. In the following, we will consider this question for the case of class types.

Recall that class types are generated from the grammar:

$$\text{TYPE} ::= \text{Void} \mid \text{Int} \mid \text{Bool} \mid \uparrow\text{C}$$

With such types we can specify some, but far from all, sets of classes. In the "types as sets of classes" perspective, we can interpret these type expressions a follows:

- the expression Void specifies the *empty set*;
- the expressions Int and Bool specify the sets {Int} and {Bool}; and
- the expression ↑C specifies the cone with root C.

If we were working under a closed-world assumption, then the type expressions could be expanded into finite sets of classes, and the usual type rules from Section 4.3 would apply. Under an open-world assumption, however, the cone sets become infinite since a class has an unbounded number of potential subclasses. With infinite sets, it is in general not clear how to decide the type constraints. Thus, we must use the special properties of just these expressions to develop a type-checking algorithm.

A crucial ingredient is the ability to decide the subclassing relation between classes occurring in the program. This can of course be done on the basis of the **inherits** parts. It follows that we can decide set inclusion among our types.

The requirements for all possible combinations are shown in this table.

$\subseteq$	Void	Int	Bool	$\uparrow$C
Void	*true*	*true*	*true*	*true*
Int	*false*	*true*	*false*	*false*
Bool	*false*	*false*	*true*	*false*
$\uparrow$D	*false*	*false*	*false*	$D \leq C$

The meaning of the notation $D \leq C$ is: D is either C itself, or it is a subclass of C, or it is a subclass of a subclass of C, and so on.

The situation in the case of $\uparrow$D and $\uparrow$C is illustrated below. The set $\uparrow$D is contained in $\uparrow$C exactly when D belongs to set $\uparrow$C.

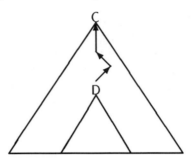

We also need to compute intersections of class types. The only non-trivial case is $\uparrow$C $\cap$ $\uparrow$D = $\uparrow$D if $D \leq C$. Unions of class types are not always possible; for example, the union of two cone sets need not be a cone set.

4.6.2 Derived Type Constraints

We now derive typing rules for class types, by specializing the 22 different type constraints from Section 4.3. The specialization proceeds by projecting the general sets to those that can be denoted by class types. This naturally leads to some restrictions, see cases 14) and 19).

1) "INT". For any integer constant k we have the constraint·

$$[\![k]\!] = \text{Int}$$

2) "true" and "false". For the boolean constants we have the constraints:

$$[\![\text{true}]\!] = \text{Bool} \quad \text{and} \quad [\![\text{false}]\!] = \text{Bool}$$

3) "nil". For the nil constant we have the constraint:

$$[\![\text{nil}]\!] = \text{Void}$$

4) "EXP_1 + EXP_2". For the addition, the constraints are:

$$[\![\text{EXP}_1]\!] = \text{Int}$$
$$[\![\text{EXP}_2]\!] = \text{Int}$$
$$[\![\text{EXP}_1 + \text{EXP}_2]\!] = \text{Int}$$

The cases 5)–11) are entirely similar to case 4). Hence, they are omitted.

12) "$\text{ID} := \text{EXP}$". For the assignment, the constraints are:

$$[\![\text{EXP}]\!] \subseteq [\![\text{ID}]\!]$$
$$[\![\text{ID} := \text{EXP}]\!] = [\![\text{EXP}]\!]$$

13) "EXP_1 ; EXP_2". For the sequence, the constraint is:

$$[\![\text{EXP}_1 \; ; \; \text{EXP}_2]\!] = [\![\text{EXP}_2]\!]$$

14) "**if** EXP_1 **then** EXP_2 **else** EXP_3 **end**". Since we cannot form unions of class types, we must require the two branches to have the same type. Thus, the constraints become:

$$[\![\text{EXP}_1]\!] = \text{Bool}$$
$$[\![\textbf{if } \text{EXP}_1 \textbf{ then } \text{EXP}_2 \textbf{ else } \text{EXP}_3 \textbf{ end}]\!] = [\![\text{EXP}_2]\!] = [\![\text{EXP}_3]\!]$$

15) "**while** EXP_1 **do** EXP_2 **end**". For the iteration, the constraints are:

$$[\![\text{EXP}_1]\!] = \text{Bool}$$
$$[\![\textbf{while } \text{EXP}_1 \textbf{ do } \text{EXP}_2 \textbf{ end}]\!] = \text{Void}$$

16) "**self**". The constraint for the **self** meta-variable is:

$$[\![\textsf{self-C}]\!] = \text{C}$$

17) "ID **new**". The constraint for object creation is:

$$[\![\text{ID } \textbf{new}]\!] = \text{ID}$$

18) "EXP **class new**". The constraints for the indirect object creation are:

$$[\![\text{EXP}]\!] \subseteq \{\textit{all classes}\}$$
$$[\![\text{EXP } \textbf{class new}]\!] = [\![\text{EXP}]\!]$$

The first constraint can also be decided for class types. It holds if $[\![\text{EXP}]\!]$ is a cone.

19) "EXP **instance-of** $\uparrow\text{ID}$". The constraint for the dynamic check of class membership is:

$$[\![\text{EXP } \textbf{instance-of } \uparrow\text{ID}]\!] = \uparrow\text{ID}$$

where we restrict the possible checks to cone sets.

20) "ID". For a variable or a formal argument, we have the constraint:

$$\llbracket \text{ID} \rrbracket = \textit{the declared type}$$

21) This constraint is one of those given for message sends.

$$\llbracket \text{EXP} \rrbracket \subseteq \{ \textit{all legal receiver classes} \}$$

This constraint is false if $\llbracket \text{EXP} \rrbracket$ is Void, Int, or Bool. If $\llbracket \text{EXP} \rrbracket = {\uparrow}\text{C}$ for some class C, then the requirement for being a legal receiver class is that a method named ID which accepts n arguments is implemented. This holds for all classes in ${\uparrow}\text{C}$ if and only if it holds for C, provided methods cannot be canceled in subclasses.

22) This is the final constraint for message sends:

$$\text{C} \in \llbracket \text{EXP} \rrbracket \Rightarrow \begin{cases} \llbracket \text{EXP}_1 \rrbracket \subseteq \llbracket \text{ID}_1 \rrbracket \\ \quad \vdots \\ \llbracket \text{EXP}_n \rrbracket \subseteq \llbracket \text{ID}_n \rrbracket \\ \llbracket \text{EXP . ID (EXP}_1, \ldots, \text{EXP}_n \text{)} \rrbracket \supseteq \text{TYPE} \supseteq \llbracket \text{EXP}_0 \rrbracket \end{cases}$$

Suppose $\llbracket \text{EXP} \rrbracket$ is a cone set of the form ${\uparrow}\text{D}$ for some class D. The condition $\text{C} \in \llbracket \text{EXP} \rrbracket$ can then be verified by checking that C is a subclass of D.

Insertion of dynamic checks is merely a question of computing intersections of types and deciding whether they are non-empty.

The type rules for SIMULA, C++, and EIFFEL are essentially like those above. The most important differences among them are explained in the following. A discussion of typing rules for genericity constructs is given in Chapter 7.

Consider first the rules for assignment (12) and message sends (22). SIMULA, C++, and EIFFEL differ in how they treat situations in which the required inclusions does not hold.

SIMULA has the same strategy as BOPL for inserting dynamic checks. The syntax for a dynamic check is EXP **qua** ID, and it has the same meaning as our **instance-of**. The **qua**-checks can be inserted explicitly by the programmer or implicitly be the compiler.

In C++, there are both types of *objects* and of *pointers* to objects. For objects, the rule for assignment requires the usual inclusion to hold. For pointers to objects, it is enough that the left- and right-hand classes are on the same path in the subclass hierarchy. Thus, dynamic checks are omitted from dangerous situations; the responsibility rests with the programmer. Dynamic checks are even impossible, since objects for reasons of compatibility with C *structs* do not include a class identification.

EIFFEL simply rejects assignments and message sends that do not satisfy the required inclusions. There are no implicit dynamic checks, but it has been proposed that a *reverse assignment* written b?=a is allowed when the type of b is a subset of that of a. If the assignment cannot happen successfully, then a run-time error is provoked.

Consider then the rule for the nil constant (3). In SIMULA and BETA, there is no type corresponding to Void. Still, the nil constant, which is written none, can be assigned to variables of all class types. Thus, it is implicitly assumed that nil has a type which is a subset of all other types.

It is unreasonable to explain nil as an instance of some class, say NoClass. The reason is that if we have an assignment "ID := nil", where ID is of type ↑C, then we must require that NoClass is a subclass of C. Hence, NoClass should then be a subclass of all other classes! This requires a strange form of multiple inheritance where NoClass inherits all code ever written, and where the only instance of NoClass (nil) does not understand any messages! We conclude that Void is the appropriate type of nil.

In C++, the nil constant is just the usual null from C. In EIFFEL, there is no universal nil constant. Rather, all types include a special value, Void, which is the initial value of its variables. The condition b.Void decides whether the variable b contains this initial value. Thus, there is no need for a Void type.

Bibliographical Notes

The idea of using sets of classes as types was first suggested by Johnson [34] and later explored by Graver and Johnson [28, 27]. Such types has much in common with the information that the SELF system collects at run-time for optimization purposes [32].

The constraint technique goes at back at least to the beginning of the 1980s. For an introduction in a λ-calculus setting, see the paper by Wand [69]. The constraint technique was first applied to an object-oriented language in our paper [55].

Vitek, Horspool, and Uhl [68] demonstrated how to extend the constraint technique with data flow analysis.

Insertion of dynamic type checks in BETA is explained in [42]. The typing rules for C++ are explained in [23]. The typing rules for EIFFEL are explained in [45].

The concept of *subtyping* originates from the type system of SIMULA. Since classes are used as types in SIMULA, a subclass is also called a subtype. With the generalization from class types to arbitrary sets, subtyping becomes something on its own. One type is a subtype of another if it is a subset of the other. Thus, subtyping is set inclusion. Another way to look at this is to first define subtyping as set inclusion and then observe that in the case of class types, subtyping is the same as subclassing.

Exercises

1. Describe the semantics of the following novel BOPL expressions:

   a) **repeat** EXP_1 **until** EXP_2 **end**
   b) **for** ID:=EXP_1 **to** EXP_2 **do** EXP_3 **end**

   Give for each expression the appropriate type constraints and extend the type checking algorithm TC to handle them.
2. Imagine that BOPL is extended with the type **Real**. Extend the type constraints on arithmetic operators such that they become overloaded on integers and reals.
3. Redo exercise 2 under the assumption that integer values can be implicitly coerced into real values. Thus, 4+3.17 will be type correct and yield a value of type **Real**.
4. Describe a possible semantics of the following novel BOPL expression:

```
typecase EXP
    TYPE₁ => EXP₁
    TYPE₂ => EXP₂
    ...
    TYPE₁ => EXP₁
end
```

   Give the appropriate type constraints and extend the type checking algorithm TC to handle them.
5. Consider the following program. Derive its type constraints and find their minimal solution.

```
class X
    var j: Int
    method dec(i: Int) returns Int
        i−j
    end
    method fac(n: Int) returns Int
        if n = 0 then
            1
        else
            j := 1;
            n*self.fac(self.dec(n))
        end
    end
end

(X new).fac(7)
```

6. Consider the following program. Derive its type constraints and show that they have no solution. Insert the required dynamic checks. Is the program dynamically type correct?

```
class Y
    var a: {Int, Bool}
    method m(b: Int) returns Bool
        if b = 0 then
            a
        else
            self.m(b-1)
        end
    end
end
```

   (Y new).m(87)

7. Assume that the set of integer values is a subset of the real values. Extend the table in Section 4.6.1 (for deciding subset inclusion) to reflect this.

8. Consider the following type system:

   TYPE ::= Void | Int | Bool | [IDLIST?]

   A type of the form [Init,Push,Pop] denotes the set of classes that implement at least methods named Init, Push, and Pop. Derive the type constraints and subtyping rules for such types.

9. Consider the following extension of the type system based on class types:

   TYPE ::= Void | Int | Bool | ↑C | @C

   The new type @C denotes the singleton set containing only the class C. Derive the type constraints and subtyping rules for such types.

10. Consider the following extension of the type system based on class types:

   TYPE ::= Void | Int | Bool | ↑C | TYPE + TYPE

   The new operator + means "set union". We will call such types *union types*. Examples of union types are Int+Bool, Void+↑D, and ↑C+↑D+↑E. Derive the type constraints and subtyping rules for union types and describe how set inclusion, union, and intersection can be computed.

11. Discuss the usefulness of the type system in exercise 4.8. Consider extensions of it, where requirements to the arguments of methods are also described in the type expressions.

12. Argue that the algorithm for inserting dynamic checks is *idempotent*, i.e., two applications yield the same result as one.

13. Consider an extension of BOPL in which a value may also be a *pair* of values. This resembles the situation with structs in C++. Expressions are extended with:

$$\text{EXP} \quad ::= \quad \mathsf{pair}(\text{EXP},\text{EXP}) \mid \mathsf{fst}(\text{EXP}) \mid \mathsf{snd}(\text{EXP})$$

and types are extended with:

$$\text{TOKEN} ::= \text{TOKEN} \times \text{TOKEN}$$

denoting pair tokens. Give the appropriate type constraints for this extension.

14. On top of exercise 4.13 we can define type expressions as:

$$\text{TYPE} \quad ::= \quad \text{TYPE} \times \text{TYPE}$$

denoting pair types. Show how to expand such type expressions into sets of (pair) tokens.

15. What does your type rules from exercise 4.13 say about the following declarations and assignment?

> **var** x: $A \times B$
> **var** y: A
> **var** z: B
>
> y := fst(pair(A **new**, z))

16. In the framework of exercise 4.13, can you find a type for the variable x such that:

> x := pair(x, 7)

is statically type correct?

17. The language of exercise 4.13 can be extended such that message sends are *broadcasted* to the individual components of pairs. For example, the expression:

> pair(x, y).m(true)

is equivalent to:

> pair(x.m(true), y.m(true))

Show how to modify the type constraints to reflect broadcasting. Modify the type checking algorithm TC to handle these constraints.

5

Type Inference

This chapter advocates the use of type inference in object-oriented languages; explains how the type inference problem naturally arises from our previous description of type checking; presents an abstract way of doing type inference and gives a concrete, efficient algorithm; describes how to avoid inferring types for the unused parts of a large class library; introduces the ideas of copying code to obtain more precise type information; and finally relates our type inference approach to the type systems based on class types.

5.1 Why Type Inference?

Type inference may be helpful both for languages that do not allow type annotations and for those that do. This section explains why.

5.1.1 SMALLTALK *is Dynamically Typed*

Some object-oriented languages do not allow type annotations to be specified in programs. A notable example is SMALLTALK where variables are declared simply by listing their names. During the execution of a SMALLTALK program, every object has a pointer to its class; this class may be thought of as a type of the object. When a message is sent to an object, it is checked if the class (or one of the superclasses) implements a method for the message. In other words, it is checked if the object has an appropriate type. For this reason, SMALLTALK and related languages are said to be *dynamically* typed.

SMALLTALK has no type inference algorithm, although several attempts has been made to provide one. It is of course possible to give a trivial algorithm that rejects all programs, but so far no algorithm has appeared that is able to infer types in most common SMALLTALK programs. A type inference algorithm would yield considerable benefits, however. It need not *annotate* SMALLTALK programs; the inferred information can still yield the safety and optimization benefits. This means that for the SMALLTALK programmer, the language need

not change at all; what changes is the arsenal of tools at his disposal. For
the programmer, it is of course immaterial if the safety checker or the code
generator uses information produced by type inference.

A type inference algorithm can take advantage of not having to annotate
programs. For example, it could use types that would be completely
unintelligible if printed, or it could transform the program text in semantics
preserving ways that allow the inference of more precise types. The latter idea
will be exploited later in this chapter.

5.1.2   From Prototype to Product

The explicit type annotations in languages like SIMULA, C++, and EIFFEL
are helpful as documentation of completed programs. They can also serve as
partial specifications during program development and as contracts between
separately developed program parts. During the early stages of program
development, however, it may be considered too cumbersome to provide type
annotations. Perhaps type correctness is not important at that stage, and
perhaps the first prototypes of the program are executed by an interpreter
that does not use the type annotations anyway. The fundamental dichotomy
is that although programs without type annotations are concise and flexible,
the finished product may have to be written in an explicitly typed language
to get efficiency and a safety guarantee.

Type inference can help smooth the transition from an untyped prototype
to a typed product, as illustrated below.

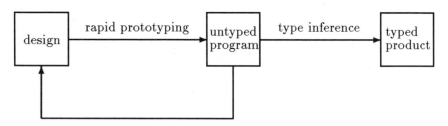

By analogy, the process may be like developing the syntax of a language.
During the early stages of development, the focus is on getting the grammar
right, and only towards the end is it important to obtain, for example, a
LALR(1) grammar acceptable to YACC.

A type inference algorithm does not know the intentions of programmers
and may infer unexpected types. For example, if a piece of program is more
general than the programmer imagined, then the inferred type need not be
what the programmer would have written in an explicitly typed language.

In this chapter we will consider type inference for BOPL programs, where
types are finite sets of classes. More specifically, the only classes that can

appear in a type are those that are written in the program at hand. Thus, we infer types under the closed-world assumption. This has the benefit of yielding more precise types than with an open-world assumption and, as explained later in this chapter, the class types used with an open-word assumption can still be recovered.

5.2   From Type Checking to Type Inference

Our approach to type inference has a simple interface to our approach to type checking: the constraints. This section reviews the difficulties faced by type inference, explains why the constraints introduced in the previous chapter yields a good starting point for type inference, and chooses a subset of the constraints that will used by our type inference algorithm.

5.2.1   Why is Type Inference Difficult?

There are three reasons why type inference for object-oriented languages is difficult:

- late binding;
- recursion; and
- inheritance.

Let us briefly examine each of them in turn. The construct of late binding encourages a programming style where the "type" of a piece of program text depends on its context. Consider for example the following method.

```
method TransPrint(g)
  g.Translate(100,200);
  g.Print;
  g
end
```

The body of this method works for all arguments that can respond to a Translate and a Print message. Though this method might have been written with the purpose of accepting a certain family of arguments, it can of course be invoked with unforeseen arguments. Thus, from an abstract view, this code may have completely different "types", depending on the context in which it is used.

The recursion used by object-oriented programs makes it difficult for a type inference algorithm to follow the flow of information. Objects send messages to themselves and back and forth to other objects. Together with late binding, this yields a type inference problem that seems qualitatively different from what is found in other programming paradigms.

The construct of inheritance further magnifies the problems faced by a type inference algorithm. Inheritance allows code, written for one purpose, to be slightly modified and used for another purpose. As with late binding, this means that typing is context-dependent.

In this chapter we concentrate on inferring types in the BOPL language without inheritance, since the problems due to late binding and recursion are the fundamental ones. Once they are solved, it is a minor task to extend the solution to handle inheritance; this is elaborated further in the bibliographical notes.

5.2.2   Choosing the Constraints

In the previous chapter on type checking, we demonstrated how to generate a set of type constraints from a program text. The emphasis there was on *checking* that the explicit type annotations yield a solution of these constraints. When the type annotations are absent, there is no solution to check, but we can of course still generate the rest of the constraints. Our approach to type inference is to *solve* these constraints, and then extract type information from the solution.

Programs need not be either fully typed or completely without annotations. We will consider the general problem where some annotations may be provided, but perhaps not all. This emphasizes that the process of checking a solution is a special case of computing a solution. For example, consider the following PASCAL program.

```
var x,y: Integer;
var z;

writeln(x+y);
z[87] := true;
```

In the previous chapter we considered a version of this program where z was explicitly annotated. The constraints for the new version of the program are the same as those for the old version, except that the one from the annotation of z is missing and except that we have omitted the array size from the array type.

$$[\![x]\!] = \text{Integer}$$
$$[\![y]\!] = \text{Integer}$$
$$[\![x]\!] = [\![y]\!]$$
$$[\![x]\!] = \text{Integer} \Rightarrow [\![x+y]\!] = \text{Integer}$$
$$[\![x]\!] = \text{Real} \Rightarrow [\![x+y]\!] = \text{Real}$$
$$[\![87]\!] = \text{Integer}$$
$$[\![\text{true}]\!] = \text{Boolean}$$

$$[\![z[87]]\!] = [\![\textbf{true}]\!]$$
$$[\![z]\!] = \textbf{array of } [\![z[87]]\!]$$

These constraints are clearly solvable, and in particular we find that z must have the type **array of** Boolean. This information could then be used to annotate the declaration of z.

For the BOPL language, the constraints will be modified slightly before we attempt to solve them. This allows us to view the problem abstractly in a simple framework. We want all constraints to look like one of these:

$$C \subseteq X \qquad \textit{start constraints}$$
$$X \subseteq Y \qquad \textit{propagation constraints}$$
$$c \in X \Rightarrow Y \subseteq Z \qquad \textit{conditional constraints}$$

where X, Y, and Z are type variables, c is a token, and C is a set of tokens. As we shall see in Section 5.3, a system of such constraints have a unique minimal solution. This means that we can compute the "best" type annotations specified by the constraints.

The most glaring omission from our list are those of the form:

$$X \subseteq C \qquad \textit{safety constraints}$$

which place upper bounds on type variables. However, if we have a system that includes constraints of this form, then we can remove them, compute the minimal solution of the remaining constraints, and verify the safety constraints afterwards. In other words, safety constraints do not contribute positively to solutions.

Recall that our type checking algorithm is capable of inserting run-time checks into potentially unsafe programs. We will take advantage of this in of our type inference algorithm, by designing it to infer as *small* sets as possible for *all* programs. The annotated program can then be submitted to the type checker, which will attempt to verify the safety constraints and insert run-time checks as required.

5.2.3 Type Constraints

In this section, we review the constraints from Section 4.3.3 and bring them into the form in which we shall submit them to the type inference algorithm.

1) "INT". For any integer constant k we have the constraint:

$$[\![k]\!] \supseteq \{\mathsf{Int}\}$$

Here, we have simply removed the safety part of the constraint.

2) "true" and "false". For the boolean constants we have the constraints:

$$\llbracket \text{true} \rrbracket \supseteq \{\text{Bool}\} \quad \text{and} \quad \llbracket \text{false} \rrbracket \supseteq \{\text{Bool}\}$$

Again, the safety part has been removed.

3) "nil". No constraints are necessary.

4) "EXP_1 + EXP_2". For the addition, the constraint is:

$$\llbracket \text{EXP}_1 + \text{EXP}_2 \rrbracket \supseteq \{\text{Int}\}$$

since safety constraints are omitted. The cases 5)–11) are similar to case 4); hence they are omitted.

12) "$\text{ID} := \text{EXP}$". For the assignment, the constraints are:

$$\llbracket \text{EXP} \rrbracket \subseteq \llbracket \text{ID} \rrbracket$$
$$\llbracket \text{ID} := \text{EXP} \rrbracket \supseteq \llbracket \text{EXP} \rrbracket$$

We have left out the constraint $\llbracket \text{ID} := \text{EXP} \rrbracket \subseteq \llbracket \text{EXP} \rrbracket$. This yields the same minimal solution, since no other constraints contribute to $\llbracket \text{ID} := \text{EXP} \rrbracket$.

13) "EXP_1 ; EXP_2". For the sequence, the constraint is:

$$\llbracket \text{EXP}_1 ; \text{EXP}_2 \rrbracket \supseteq \llbracket \text{EXP}_2 \rrbracket$$

Again, the equality can safely be weakened to an inclusion.

14) "**if** EXP_1 **then** EXP_2 **else** EXP_3 **end**". For the conditional, the constraints are:

$$\llbracket \text{EXP}_1 \rrbracket \supseteq \{\text{Bool}\}$$
$$\llbracket \textbf{if } \text{EXP}_1 \textbf{ then } \text{EXP}_2 \textbf{ else } \text{EXP}_3 \textbf{ end} \rrbracket \supseteq \llbracket \text{EXP}_2 \rrbracket$$
$$\llbracket \textbf{if } \text{EXP}_1 \textbf{ then } \text{EXP}_2 \textbf{ else } \text{EXP}_3 \textbf{ end} \rrbracket \supseteq \llbracket \text{EXP}_3 \rrbracket$$

As for cases 12) and 13), the equality is replaced by an inclusion, which allows the set union to be split into two independent constraints.

15) "**while** EXP_1 **do** EXP_2 **end**". For the iteration, the constraints are:

$$\llbracket \text{EXP}_1 \rrbracket \supseteq \{\text{Bool}\}$$

The safety constraint is omitted, as is the constraint on the entire **while**-expression.

16) "**self**". The constraint for the **self** meta-variable is:

$$\llbracket \text{self-C} \rrbracket \supseteq \{\text{C}\}$$

where the safety constraint is omitted.

17) "ID **new**". The constraint for object creation is:

$$\llbracket \text{ID } \textbf{new} \rrbracket \supseteq \{\text{ID}\}$$

where the safety constraint is omitted.

18) "EXP **class new**". The constraint for the indirect object creation is:

$$[\![\text{EXP } \textbf{class new}]\!] \supseteq [\![\text{EXP}]\!]$$

where the safety constraint is omitted.

19) "EXP **instance-of** {IDLIST}". The constraint for the dynamic check of class membership is:

$$[\![\text{EXP } \textbf{instance-of} \ \{\ \text{IDLIST}\ \}]\!] \supseteq \{\ \text{IDLIST}\ \}$$

where the safety constraint is omitted.

20) "ID". For a variable or a formal argument with a type annotation, we have the constraint:

$$[\![\text{ID}]\!] \supseteq \textit{the declared type}$$

where the safety constraint is omitted.

21) For message sends, we omit the constraint that checks legality.

22) The conditional constraints for message sends are:

$$C \in [\![\text{EXP}]\!] \Rightarrow \left\{ \begin{array}{l} [\![\text{EXP}_1]\!] \subseteq [\![\text{ID}_1]\!] \\ \quad \vdots \\ [\![\text{EXP}_n]\!] \subseteq [\![\text{ID}_n]\!] \\ [\![\text{EXP . ID (EXP}_1, \ldots, \text{EXP}_n \text{)}]\!] \supseteq [\![\text{EXP}_0]\!] \end{array} \right.$$

The declared result type is ignored.

In the following section we show an abstract way of solving such constraints.

5.3   Solving Constraints

When each constraint is on one of the three forms discussed in the previous section, then the constraint system has a minimal solution. This section explains why and gives two examples.

5.3.1   The Existence of a Minimal Solution

Each type variable ranges over the family of all possible types, that is, the family of all possible finite sets of tokens. This family is ordered by set inclusion, so the smallest type is the empty set and the largest type, called $\mathcal{U}$, is the set containing all classes in the program. The family of possible types and its ordering can be illustrated as follows.

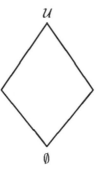

The task of type inference is to assign elements of this family to all type variables such that all constraints are satisfied. This means that each possible solution is a tuple of types, with one entry for each type variable. Such tuples are ordered by point-wise set inclusion, so that the smallest possible solution is the one that assigns the empty set to all type variables. The family of possible solutions of a constraint system can be illustrated as follows.

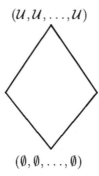

If more than one solution of a constraint system exists, then we will have to choose between the possible ones. Our guide in this matter is that we want as small a solution as possible.

Recall that we have omitted the safety constraints. Intuitively, this means that we ignore errors. Thus, intuitively, the remaining constraints should have a solution. Indeed, this is the case. Consider the top element of the family of solutions. Clearly all constraints are then satisfied, since we can substitute $\mathcal{U}$ for every variable:

$$C \subseteq \mathcal{U}$$
$$\mathcal{U} \subseteq \mathcal{U}$$
$$c \in \mathcal{U} \Rightarrow \mathcal{U} \subseteq \mathcal{U}$$

The upside of this is that we can guarantee that types can be inferred for all programs. The downside is that this maximal solution is useless because it simply says that all expressions will evaluate to *something*, unless they loop or yield an error.

There may be more than one solution to a constraint system. As part of our search for a minimal solution, we will now show that solutions are *closed under point-wise intersection*. The meaning of this is that if $\mathcal{L}$ and $\mathcal{M}$ are two solutions of a constraint system, for example:

$$\begin{aligned} \mathcal{L} &= (L_1, L_2, \ldots, L_n) \\ \mathcal{M} &= (M_1, M_2, \ldots, M_n) \end{aligned}$$

then we can construct a possibly new solution, written $\mathcal{L} \sqcap \mathcal{M}$, by forming:

$$\mathcal{L} \sqcap \mathcal{M} = (L_1 \cap M_1, L_2 \cap M_2, \ldots, L_n \cap M_n)$$

To see that this is a solution, let us consider each of the three forms of constraints in turn. Suppose the values for the type variables X, Y, Z are contained in the i'th, j'th, and k'th place of a solution tuple, respectively. First, consider a constraint of the form $C \subseteq X$. Since $\mathcal{L}$ and $\mathcal{M}$ are solutions, we get that $C \subseteq L_i$ and $C \subseteq M_i$. Clearly, also $C \subseteq (L_i \cap M_i)$.

Second, consider a constraint of the form $X \subseteq Y$. Since $\mathcal{L}$ and $\mathcal{M}$ are solutions, we get that $L_i \subseteq L_j$ and $M_i \subseteq M_j$. Clearly, we have that $(L_i \cap M_i) \subseteq (L_j \cap M_j)$.

Third, consider a constraint of the form $c \in X \Rightarrow Y \subseteq Z$. Since $\mathcal{L}$ and $\mathcal{M}$ are solutions, we get that $c \in L_i \Rightarrow L_j \subseteq L_k$ and $c \in M_i \Rightarrow M_j \subseteq M_k$. We must show that $c \in (L_i \cap M_i) \Rightarrow (L_j \cap M_j) \subseteq (L_k \cap M_k)$. To do this, suppose $c \in (L_i \cap M_i)$. Clearly, also $c \in L_i$ and $c \in M_i$, so also $L_j \subseteq L_k$ and $M_j \subseteq M_k$. Hence, $(L_j \cap M_j) \subseteq (L_k \cap M_k)$, as required.

We have now shown that solutions are closed under point-wise intersection. This may at first seem somewhat in vain, since the only solution we so far know of is the top element of the solution space—a completely uninteresting solution. Although we as yet do not *know* of other solutions, we can *imagine* the family of all solutions of a given constraint system. This set may be large, but it is *finite* since the family of all possible solutions is finite. Let us enumerate all the solutions:

$$\mathcal{L}_1, \mathcal{L}_2, \ldots, \mathcal{L}_m$$

and recall that we write the point-wise intersection as $\sqcap$. We can then use $\sqcap$ to form a possible solution $\mathcal{L}_*$:

$$\mathcal{L}_* = \mathcal{L}_1 \sqcap \mathcal{L}_2 \sqcap \ldots \sqcap \mathcal{L}_m$$

Clearly, $\sqcap$ is associative so we have omitted parentheses. The point of constructing $\mathcal{L}_*$ is that it itself is a solution of the constraints! To see this, recall that all of the $\mathcal{L}_i$'s are solutions, and when $\sqcap$ are applied to two solutions, then the result is a new solution. Thus, $\mathcal{L}_*$ is somewhere in the family $\mathcal{L}_1, \mathcal{L}_2, \ldots, \mathcal{L}_m$. Moreover, $\mathcal{L}_*$ is smaller than or equal to every member of this family. This is because $\sqcap$ constructs a possible solution which is smaller than or equal to its arguments.

To sum up, we have shown that there is a minimal solution of every constraint system. Along the way, we have shown that it can be computed by constructing all assignments of sets to variables, filtering out all the solutions, and computing their intersection. This demonstrates that the minimal solution is computable.

This particular algorithm is of course unacceptably slow. If n is the size of a program text, then there are $O(n)$ type variables and $O(n)$ classes, hence $O((2^n)^n)$ possible solutions. We need not go into further details: the naïve algorithm runs in at least exponential time.

Since the minimal solution is computable, it cannot always yield the optimal type information about a program—the one that captures the actual run-time behavior. The optimal information can in general only be obtained by observing all possible executions of the program and recording the actual values involved.

The computable information is point-wise greater than the optimal type information. This reflects that *all* the desired type information is contained in the minimal solution, but some extra tokens may be included. Thus, the minimal solution is a conservative approximation. Conversely, the optimal information will not always be a solution of the constraints. The relationship between the computable and the optimal information can be illustrated as follows.

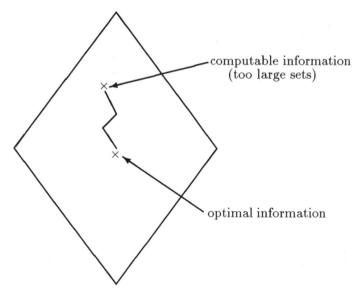

computable information
(too large sets)

optimal information

5.3.2 Examples

We will now reconsider two example programs from Section 4.3.4, but this time without type annotations.

Consider first a version of the small nonsense program introduced in Section 4.3.1.

```
class A
    var x
    var y
    method m(f)
        f.m(x)
    end
end

class B
    method m(g)
        self
    end
end
```

$$(A \ \textbf{new}).m(B \ \textbf{new}).m(nil)$$

Below is the collection of constraints that are generated according to the rules in Section 5.2.3. For each constraint, we have indicated its origin using the above enumeration of the general constraints.

$$22) \quad A \in \llbracket f \rrbracket \Rightarrow \begin{cases} \llbracket x \rrbracket \subseteq \llbracket f \rrbracket \\ \llbracket f.m(x) \rrbracket \supseteq \llbracket f.m(x) \rrbracket \end{cases}$$

$$22) \quad B \in \llbracket f \rrbracket \Rightarrow \begin{cases} \llbracket x \rrbracket \subseteq \llbracket g \rrbracket \\ \llbracket f.m(x) \rrbracket \supseteq \llbracket \text{self-B} \rrbracket \end{cases}$$

$$16) \quad \llbracket \text{self-B} \rrbracket \supseteq \{B\}$$

$$17) \quad \llbracket A \ \textbf{new} \rrbracket \supseteq \{A\}$$

$$17) \quad \llbracket B \ \textbf{new} \rrbracket \supseteq \{B\}$$

$$22) \quad A \in \llbracket A \ \textbf{new} \rrbracket \Rightarrow \begin{cases} \llbracket B \ \textbf{new} \rrbracket \subseteq \llbracket f \rrbracket \\ \llbracket (A \ \textbf{new}).m(B \ \textbf{new}) \rrbracket \supseteq \llbracket f.m(x) \rrbracket \end{cases}$$

$$22) \quad B \in \llbracket A \ \textbf{new} \rrbracket \Rightarrow \begin{cases} \llbracket B \ \textbf{new} \rrbracket \subseteq \llbracket g \rrbracket \\ \llbracket (A \ \textbf{new}).m(B \ \textbf{new}) \rrbracket \supseteq \llbracket \text{self-B} \rrbracket \end{cases}$$

$$22) \quad A \in \llbracket (A \ \textbf{new}).m(B \ \textbf{new}) \rrbracket \Rightarrow$$
$$\begin{cases} \llbracket nil \rrbracket \subseteq \llbracket f \rrbracket \\ \llbracket (A \ \textbf{new}).m(B \ \textbf{new}).m(nil) \rrbracket \supseteq \llbracket f.m(x) \rrbracket \end{cases}$$

$$22) \quad B \in \llbracket (A \ \textbf{new}).m(B \ \textbf{new}) \rrbracket \Rightarrow$$
$$\begin{cases} \llbracket nil \rrbracket \subseteq \llbracket g \rrbracket \\ \llbracket (A \ \textbf{new}).m(B \ \textbf{new}).m(nil) \rrbracket \supseteq \llbracket \text{self-B} \rrbracket \end{cases}$$

The minimal solution of this constraint system is as follows.

$$[\![x]\!] = \{\}$$
$$[\![y]\!] = \{\}$$
$$[\![f]\!] = \{B\}$$
$$[\![g]\!] = \{\}$$
$$[\![f.m(x)]\!] = \{B\}$$
$$[\![self\text{-}B]\!] = \{B\}$$
$$[\![A\ \textbf{new}]\!] = \{A\}$$
$$[\![B\ \textbf{new}]\!] = \{B\}$$
$$[\![(A\ \textbf{new}).m(B\ \textbf{new})]\!] = \{B\}$$
$$[\![nil]\!] = \{\}$$
$$[\![(A\ \textbf{new}).m(B\ \textbf{new}).m(nil)]\!] = \{B\}$$

This solution is smaller than that for the constraint system generated from the explicitly typed version of the program: $[\![x]\!]$, $[\![y]\!]$, and $[\![g]\!]$ are now assigned the empty set. The reason is that we have now omitted the constraints for type annotations.

Consider then the following program which in the annotated version from Section 4.3.4 was not type correct.

```
class C
    method n(i)
        i+1
    end
end


(C new).n(true)
```

Its constraints are given below.

$$\begin{array}{ll}
1) & [\![1]\!] \supseteq \{Int\} \\
4) & [\![i + 1]\!] \supseteq \{Int\} \\
17) & [\![C\ \textbf{new}]\!] \supseteq \{C\} \\
2) & [\![true]\!] \supseteq \{Bool\} \\
22) & C \in [\![C\ \textbf{new}]\!] \Rightarrow \left\{ \begin{array}{l} [\![true]\!] \subseteq [\![i]\!] \\ [\![(C\ \textbf{new}).n(true)]\!] \supseteq [\![i + 1]\!] \end{array} \right.
\end{array}$$

The minimal solution of this constraint system is:

$$[\![i]\!] = \{Bool\}$$
$$[\![1]\!] = \{Int\}$$
$$[\![i + 1]\!] = \{Int\}$$
$$[\![C\ \textbf{new}]\!] = \{C\}$$
$$[\![true]\!] = \{Bool\}$$
$$[\![(C\ \textbf{new}).n(true)]\!] = \{Int\}$$

The program will of course yield a run-time error, but this is not reflected in the constraint system, since we have omitted the safety constraints. If we use the inferred type information to annotate i with the type **Bool**, then we can submit the program to the type checker from the previous chapter. As we would expect, the program will then be rejected.

5.4   The Type Inference Algorithm

The type inference algorithm from the previous section is unacceptably slow because it considers *all* solutions, of which there may be exponentially many. We will now present a faster algorithm which works by iteratively computing increasingly better approximations to the minimal solution. The results in a worst-case running time of $O(n^3)$. The iterative strategy can be illustrated as follows.

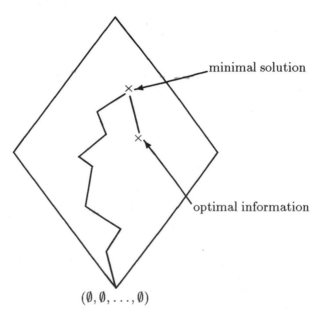

minimal solution

optimal information

$$(\emptyset, \emptyset, \dots, \emptyset)$$

The heart of the new algorithm is a data structure called SOLVER. We can insert constraints into the SOLVER, and at any time we can extract the minimal solution of the constraints inserted so far. The type inference algorithm then simply amounts to inserting all the constraints and extracting the final solution.

Notice that when more constraints are considered, the minimal solution becomes larger. Thus, the SOLVER will contain increasingly larger approximative solutions.

In the remainder of this section, we will sketch an implementation of the SOLVER such that the overall time complexity of the type inference algorithm is $O(n^3)$. The implementation uses a directed *solver* graph, in which:

- *nodes* correspond to type variables; and
- *edges* correspond to inclusions between type variables.

To each graph node is associated a set of tokens, which is the value of the corresponding type variable in the current minimal solution. In other words, if we extract the sets of classes for all type variables, then we get the minimal solution of the constraints so far inserted into the SOLVER.

We represent a set of tokens as a bitvector with an entry for each possible token. The bitvector associated with the node v is denoted $B(v)$; its i'th bit is denoted $B(v, i)$. With each entry in the bitvectors, we associate a list of constraints of the form $Y \subseteq Z$. We use this list to handle insertion of constraints of the form $c \in X \Rightarrow Y \subseteq Z$, as explained below. The list associated with the i'th bit in node v is denoted $K(v, i)$. The organization of a graph node v can be illustrated as follows.

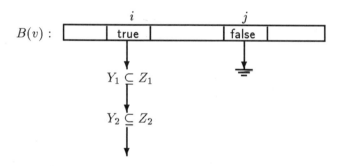

Initially, all bitvectors contain only false, and all lists are empty. The insertion of a new constraint is performed by the procedure INSERT. Inclusions are maintained by the procedure PROPAGATE which is mutually recursive with INSERT. Maintaining inclusions involves propagating bits along edges. When a bit becomes set, each constraint in the associated list is removed and inserted into the Solver.

A bit of notation is used below. The operation UNION(X,C) unions the set C to the bitvector of the graph node of X. The operation ++ concatenates two lists, and () is the empty list.

```
INSERT(C ⊆ X) =
  UNION(X,C);
  for X → Y do
    for i ∈ B(X) do
      PROPAGATE(Y,i)
    end
  end
```

```
INSERT(X ⊆ Y) =
  create an edge X → Y;
  for i ∈ B(X) do
    PROPAGATE(Y,i)
  end
INSERT(c ∈ X ⇒ Y ⊆ Z) =
  if B(X, c) then
    INSERT(Y ⊆ Z)
  else
    K(X, c) := K(X, c)++(Y ⊆ Z)
  end

PROPAGATE(v,i) =
  if ¬B(v, i) then
    B(v, i) := true;
    for v → w do
      PROPAGATE(w,i)
    end;
    for k ∈ K(v, i) do
      INSERT(k)
    end;
    K(v, i) := ()
  end
```

With this implementation of the SOLVER, the overall time complexity of the
type inference algorithm is $O(n^3)$. To see this, observe first that each bit
is propagated along an edge at most once. Since there are $O(n^2)$ edges, the
overall cost of propagation is $O(n^3)$ time. Since the remaining work is constant
for each constraint, and since there are $O(n^2)$ constraints, we arrive at $O(n^3)$
time for doing type inference.

5.5 Detecting Dead Code

Many programs contain *dead code*. This section explains why it can be
important to remove dead code, and it shows how it can be done.

5.5.1 Flow Analysis

The type inference algorithm infers types for all parts of a program. This is
convenient if we afterwards want to submit the annotated program to the type
checker. It is inefficient, however, if the main program uses only few of the

classes in the program. Moreover, if the unused program parts contain type errors, then the type checker will reject the annotated program—although these type errors cannot not cause run-time errors. The situation can be illustrated as follows.

Class Library

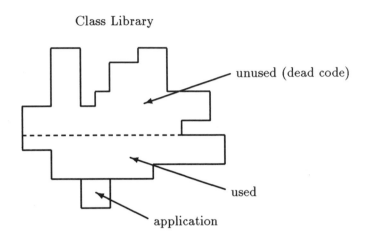

unused (dead code)

used

application

In a BOPL program, we can get the effect of having a large class library by simply including the corresponding classes in the program text. The main program is the application for which we are interested in inferring types. Those program parts that cannot be executed when running the main program are considered dead code.

It is of course uncomputable to remove *exactly* the dead parts of a program, but we may strive to remove as much as possible—as long as we never remove *live* code. To find out which code is dead, it is necessary to do a *control flow analysis*. The purpose of such an analysis is to collect information about all possible runs of the program. Those program parts that the analysis discovers to be dead can safely be removed.

Removing dead code from object-oriented programs is difficult for the same reasons that type inference is difficult: the presence of late binding, recursion, and inheritance. If we in a class C find a method m, and we elsewhere find the message send E.m, then the analysis should determine if the message send is dead, and if not, then if the method is dead.

In the following we present an algorithm that detects and removes dead code. It is a modification of our type inference algorithm.

5.5.2   The Trace Graph

To detect dead code, we use a *trace* graph.

- *Nodes* of the trace graph correspond to program parts. There is a node for the main program and a node for each method.
- *Edges* of the trace graph correspond to message sends. If a message send E.m(...) occurs in a program part that corresponds to the node N, then there is an edge from N to each node that corresponds to a method named m.

The node for the main program is called the *main* node. Each path from the main node corresponds to a potential execution of the program. Such a potential execution is called a *trace*. Thus, the trace graph is a finite representation of a possibly infinite set of traces.

The idea is to mark each node as either *dead* or *live*. Initially, only the main node is live.

The dead code detection algorithm works by solving a constraint system. The constraint system is similar to the one considered by the type inference algorithm. The difference is that each constraint may have additional conditions. Intuitively, the extra conditions reflect that only inclusions generated from live methods and from the main program are interesting. The constraint system is obtained from the trace graph as follows. For each finite path p from the main node, we generate the following constraints.

- For each edge on p, corresponding to a message send E.m(...), where m belongs to the class c, collect the condition $c \in [\![E]\!]$.
- From the method to which p leads, generate constraints as in Section 5.2.3 and add the conditions collected above.

Thus, each generated constraint is of one of the following three forms.

$$c_1 \in X_1 \wedge \ldots \wedge c_n \in X_n \quad \Rightarrow \quad C \subseteq Y$$
$$c_1 \in X_1 \wedge \ldots \wedge c_n \in X_n \quad \Rightarrow \quad Y \subseteq Z$$
$$c_1 \in X_1 \wedge \ldots \wedge c_n \in X_n \quad \Rightarrow \quad (c \in X \Rightarrow Y \subseteq Z)$$

Intuitively, such a constraint may be read as follows.

- The conditions correspond to a sequence of message sends that in the end would invoke a method m. If this sequence of message sends seems to be possible, then m is considered to be live, and thus the constraints generated from it must hold.

By generalizing the arguments of Section 5.3.1, it can be shown that such a constraint system has a minimal solution. The generated constraint system may be infinite because of loops in the trace graph. As demonstrated in the following, we can compute the minimal solution anyway.

The heart of the dead code detection algorithm is a transformed version of the SOLVER data structure from Section 5.4. This new data structure is

called the LSOLVER. We can insert the same kinds of constraints into the
LSOLVER as into the SOLVER, and we can at any time extract the minimal
solution of the constraints inserted so far. In addition, the LSOLVER keeps
track of the live methods. The set of methods that are currently marked live
can be obtained through the operation LIVE. The constraints generated from
a program fragment m are denoted CONSTRAINTS(m). The algorithm proceeds
as follows.

```
L := ∅;
for k ∈CONSTRAINTS(main) do
   INSERT(k)
end;
while L≠LIVE do
   choose m from LIVE\L;
   for k ∈CONSTRAINTS(m) do
      INSERT(k);
      L := L∪{m}
   end
end;
remove all methods not in L
```

The LSOLVER is implemented like the SOLVER, with the addition that it
maintains a bitvector representing the set of methods marked live. We let
each conditional constraint generated from rule 22) in Section 5.2.3 carry
the name of the potentially invoked method. Each insertion operation in the
LSOLVER can then maintain the set of live methods. If we insert a constraint
$c \in X \Rightarrow Y \subseteq Z$ into the LSOLVER and the condition $c \in X$ at some point
becomes satisfied, then the potentially invoked method is marked live.

Notice that a given method is marked live the first time there is a path in
the trace graph, from the main node to the node for that method, where all
the corresponding conditions are true in the current minimal solution. Such
a path will be a finite path, so the algorithm considers only finitely many
constraints when computing the minimal solution.

Clearly, the algorithm has the same time complexity as the type inference
algorithm, which is time $O(n^3)$.

The type constraints generated with dead code detection relate to the
original ones in the following way. Some constraints have been removed and
those that remain are prefixed with path conditions. Clearly, they will then
yield smaller, more precise type information. Note that any technique, which
allows the constraints to be weakened and still remain sound, will improve
type inference.

5.5.3 Example

As a simple example consider the following BOPL program.

```
class A
    method f( )
        7
    end
end

class B
    method f( )
        true
    end
end

((A new).f())+3
```

Clearly, the method f in class B is dead. The trace graph for the program looks as follows.

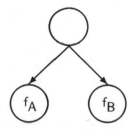

Running the dead code detection algorithm results in the removal of the dead method. Since the class B then becomes empty we can remove it as well.

```
class A
    method f( )
        7
    end
end

((A new).f())+3
```

5.6 Copying Code

The process of removing dead code, inferring types, and then type checking, may lead to the insertion of surprisingly many *unneeded* dynamic type-checks.

This section explains why and shows how two meaning-preserving program transformations can reduce the number of dynamic type-checks.

5.6.1   More Precise Constraints

Object-oriented programs usually contain *polymorphic methods* and *container classes*. A polymorphic method is one which works for several kinds of arguments. For example, a method that merely returns its argument will work for all arguments. A container class is one which is used to store different kinds of arguments. For example, a class of buffer objects allows all kinds of object to be contained in a buffer. Thus, if the buffer class defines a variable contents, then all kinds of objects can potentially be stored in contents.

Polymorphic methods and container classes both cause problems for the type inference algorithm. The problem is that there is only *one* type variable for each method argument and for each instance variable. Thus, when a polymorphic method is invoked from two different places, then the types of the arguments are unioned together. This means that the result type of both invocations are bigger than what we for each of them could have hoped for. Similarly, suppose the objects of a container class in one part of a program are used to store one family of objects and in another part are used to store a different family of objects. Clearly, the type of the instance variables in the container class will be the union of the types of the two families of objects.

To obtain a better typing of polymorphic methods and container classes we will transform the program text so that the polymorphism and the different uses of container classes becomes more explicit. Such a transformation makes the program text longer and thus yields more type variables during type inference. In the following two subsections, we show a transformation that handles polymorphic methods and another that handles container classes. Both can be iterated to yield ever better type inference results.

5.6.2   The Method Transformation

To improve the typing of polymorphic methods we create a copy of each method implementation for each syntactic invocation. The idea can be illustrated as follows.

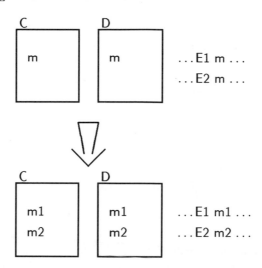

To be able to iterate the algorithm, care must be taken when choosing names for the different copies of the methods. We will not go into details with this, but merely give an example.

```
class C
    method id(x)
        x
    end
end

((C new).id(7))+10;
((C new).id(true)) or false
```

Notice that the id method gets both an integer and a boolean argument. If we do type inference, then the annotated program becomes the following.

```
class C
    method id(x: {Int, Bool} ) returns {Int, Bool}
        x
    end
end

((C new).id(7))+10;
((C new).id(true)) or false
```

This program is of course rejected by the type-checker. If we apply the method transformation to the untyped program, then we get the following.

```
class C
   method  id@1 (x)
      x
   end
   method  id@2 (x)
      x
   end
end

((C new). id@1 (7))+10;
((C new). id@2 (true)) or false
```

If we do type inference on this program, then we get the following.

```
class C
   method id@1(x: Int ) returns Int
      x
   end
   method id@2(x: Bool ) returns Bool
      x
   end
end

((C new).id@1(7))+10;
((C new).id@2(true)) or false
```

This program is accepted by the type checker (no dynamic type checks are inserted).

The method transformation may in the worst case square the size of a program. If the program was large to begin with, then this may be seem to be unacceptable price to pay for a better typing. Many of the new methods are likely to be dead, however. This means that if we after the method transformation apply dead code detection, then the program can be expected to shrink to a reasonable size.

5.6.3   The Class Transformation

To improve the typing of container classes we create a copy of each class for each syntactic new. The idea can be illustrated as follows.

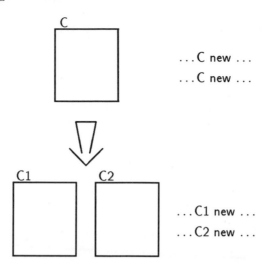

To be able to iterate the algorithm, care must be taken when choosing names for the different copies of the classes. We will not go into details with this, but merely give an example.

```
class Container
    var x
    method put(val)
        x := val;
        self
    end
    method get()
        x
    end
end

(Container new).put(7).get()+10;
(Container new).put(false).get() or true
```

Notice that both an integer and a boolean can be stored in an x variable. If we do type inference, then the annotated program becomes the following.

```
class Container
    var x: {Int, Bool}
    method put(val: {Int, Bool}) returns {Container}
        x := val;
        self
    end
```

```
            method get( ) returns ⎡{Int, Bool}⎤
                 x
            end
        end

        (Container new).put(7).get( )+10;
        (Container new).put(false).get( ) or true
```

This program is of course rejected by the type checker. If we apply the class transformation to the untyped program, then we get the following.

```
        class ⎡Container@1⎤
            var x
            method put(val)
                x := val;
                self
            end
            method get( )
                x
            end
        end

        class ⎡Container@2⎤
            var x
            method put(val)
                x := val;
                self
            end
            method get( )
                x
            end
        end

        (⎡Container@1⎤ new).put(7).get( )+10;
        (⎡Container@2⎤ new).put(false).get( ) or true
```

If we do type inference on this program, then we get the following.

```
        class Container@1
            var x: Int
            method put(val: ⎡Int⎤) returns ⎡Container@1⎤
                x := val;
                self
            end
```

```
        method get() returns  Int
            x
        end
    end


    class Container@2
        var x: Bool
        method put(val:  Bool ) returns  Container@2
            x := val;
            self
        end
        method get() returns  Bool
            x
        end
    end


    (Container@1 new).put(7).get()+10;
    (Container@2 new).put(false).get() or true
```

This program is accepted by the type checker (no dynamic type checks are inserted).

Like the method transformation, also the class transformation may square the size of a program. Again, dead code detection may considerably reduce this expansion.

5.6.4   Using Copied Code

We now discuss how the copying of source code relates to our reasons for obtaining type information.

If we focus on readability, then having multiple copies of the same method seems rather pointless. However, we may choose instead to provide multiple annotations of the same method. For example, the identity method from Section 5.6.2 could be annotated as follows.

```
    class C
        method id(x) % Int→Int & Bool→Bool
            x
        end
    end
```

The annotation is not a formal part of the program, but merely documentation for the benefit of the programmer. The different uses of this method have been inferred from the typings of its various copies.

If reliability is our main concern, then we should merely accept that better precision can be obtained when code is copied. Since both transformations preserve semantics, we know that if a transformed program will not cause run-time errors, then neither will the original one.

Finally, if we aim for efficiency, then we may actually choose to compile each copy of a method independently. It will often be the case that we can generate efficient code for each copy, but not for the original. It may even be that some copies can be inlined, while others cannot. Thus, we have the option of a time-space tradeoff.

5.7   Class Types

So far, we have considered type inference and related algorithms under a closed-world assumption. We will now show how to infer class types. This may be interesting for existing languages like SIMULA, C++, and EIFFEL for which *no* type inference algorithm exists.

Recall that class types are generated from the grammar:

$$\text{TYPE} \quad ::= \quad \text{Void} \mid \text{Int} \mid \text{Bool} \mid \uparrow\text{C}$$

We will assume that there is a top element **Object** in the class hierarchy, i.e., all classes have a common superclass. Following the inference of finite set types, we map a set S into the class type:

$$\begin{cases} \text{Void} & \text{if } S = \{\}, \text{ otherwise} \\ \text{Int} & \text{if } S = \{\text{Int}\}, \text{ otherwise} \\ \text{Bool} & \text{if } S = \{\text{Bool}\}, \text{ otherwise} \\ \uparrow\text{C} & \text{if C is the nearest common} \\ & \text{superclass of the classes in } S \end{cases}$$

Consider for example the following class hierarchy.

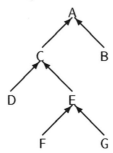

Below we show how some sets are transformed into class types.

$$\begin{aligned} \{\text{C}\} &\mapsto \uparrow\text{C} = \{\text{C}, \text{D}, \text{E}, \text{F}, \text{G}, \ldots\} \\ \{\text{D}, \text{G}\} &\mapsto \uparrow\text{C} = \{\text{C}, \text{D}, \text{E}, \text{F}, \text{G}, \ldots\} \\ \{\text{E}, \text{G}\} &\mapsto \uparrow\text{E} = \{\text{E}, \text{F}, \text{G}, \ldots\} \\ \{\text{B}\} &\mapsto \uparrow\text{B} = \{\text{B}, \ldots\} \end{aligned}$$

With this algorithm at hand, we can imagine software development in untyped versions of SIMULA, C++, and EIFFEL, where type annotations are inserted by the algorithm towards the end of a project.

Note, however, that class types are more coarse than set types. Thus, the subsequent type checking is likely to insert a great many more dynamic type checks. This is the price that is paid for supporting the open-world assumption.

Bibliographical Notes

The idea of viewing type inference as a problem of solving constraints has been explored for functional languages by Wand [69], and for imperative languages by the second author [61].

For an untyped λ-calculus, we have formulated constraints that are similar in spirit to those used in this book and we have proved the soundness of the resulting system [52]. We have also proved [52, 57] that our system accepts strictly more λ-terms than type systems based on simple types or partial types. For material on partial types, see [66, 70, 49, 37, 51].

Type inference for SMALLTALK was first addressed by Suzuki [65]. His system was unsuccessful because it pessimistically assumed that each message send may invoke all methods for that message. His approach thus lacks our conditions in the rules for message sending.

Later, a type inference system for SMALLTALK was suggested by Borning and Ingalls [5]. Their approach was unsuccessful in part because they attempted to infer class types directly, rather than using sets of classes as types.

Graver and Johnson [34, 28, 27] pioneered the "types as sets of classes" approach. They took an intermediate approach between untyped and typed in requiring the programmer to specify types for instance variables whereas types of arguments and results are inferred.

Hense [30] used a technique based on record types which are extendible and can be recursive. His technique has turned out to handle variables and assignments far less effectively than our approach [55].

The ideas of detecting dead code and copying methods was suggested by us in [55]. The idea of also copying classes were suggested by Oxhøj and us in [50].

Together with Ole Agesen [2], we have applied our type inference technique to the SELF language. This involves extending the technique to handle dynamic and multiple inheritance. Experiments with a prototype implementation demonstrated that the ideas of detecting dead code and copying code are crucial in getting reasonable running times and useful type information [2].

Exercises

1. Consider untyped versions of the programs from exercises 4.5 and 4.6. Generate their simplified constraints, find the minimal solutions, and use them to annotate the programs. Compare with the originals.
2. Simulate the workings of the SOLVER to compute the minimal solution of the following abstract constraints.

$$\{A\} \subseteq X_1$$
$$X_1 \subseteq X_2$$
$$\{B, C\} \subseteq X_3$$
$$A \in X_2 \Rightarrow X_1 \subseteq X_3$$
$$B \in X_1 \Rightarrow X_4 \subseteq X_1$$
$$X_3 \subseteq X_4$$
$$\{A, B\} \subseteq X_4$$

3. Show that the extended constraints from Section 5.2.2 always have a unique minimal solution.
4. Consider the following BOPL program.

```
class C
    method m(i)
        i+1
    end
end

(C new).m(2)
```

Write the constraints for this program and show step by step how the solver computes the minimal solution.
5. Apply the method transformation and the class transformation to the following program–first individually and then both in either order.

```
class X
    var ax
    method m(bx)
        (Y new).n(bx)
    end
    method n(cx)
        (X new).m(cx)
    end
end
```

```
class Y
  var ay
  method m(by)
    (X new).n(by)
  end
  method n(cy)
    (Y new).m(cy)
  end
end
```

```
(X new).m(Y new)
```

6. Show that applications of the method and class transformations may indeed square the size of programs.
7. Write a BOPL program that needs both the class transformation, the method transformation, and dead code removal before the inferred types yield a statically type correct program. (Use the workbench!)
8. Suggest a general principle for the multiple annotations sketched in Section 5.6.4.
9. Verify that the following classes are statically type correct.

```
class A
  method m() returns Int
    7
  end
end

class B
  method m() returns Int
    8
  end
end

class C
  var x: {A, B}
  method n() returns Int
    x.m()+1
  end
end
```

Assume that we have the following class hierarchy.

Object

A   B   C

Transform all annotations into class types, according to the technique presented in Section 5.7. Show that the program is no longer statically type correct.

10. Consider the following extension of BOPL:

    EXP   ::=   **return** EXP

    When **return** EXP is encountered, the enclosing method returns with the value of EXP. For example, the method **one** below always returns 1. Give the type constraints for **return** expressions. Perform type inference on the following program.

    ```
    class X
       method one( )
          return 1;
          true
       end
    end


    (X new).one( )
    ```

11. Consider BOPL with blocks (without arguments), as described in exercise 2.6. Give the type constraints for such blocks. How can the inferred types of a block be used to annotate the program? Perform type inference of the classes X and Y in exercise 2.6.

    Consider next blocks with arguments. Give the type constraints for such blocks, assuming they cannot be nested. Perform type inference of the class Z in exercise 2.6. What problems arise if blocks can be both nested and have arguments?

12. Consider the extension with pairs suggested in exercise 4.13. Show that the lattice of types is no longer finite. Does this have consequences for type inference?

13. The problems in 5.12 can be remedied by abandoning pair tokens and instead introducing a special token for each syntactic occurrence of a **pair** constructor. To be concrete, we can number them all and use π_i as the token for the i'th occurrence. The constraints for **pair** and **fst** are now:

$$\{\pi_i\} \subseteq [\![\mathsf{pair}(\mathrm{EXP}_1,\mathrm{EXP}_2)]\!]$$
$$\pi_i \in [\![\mathrm{EXP}]\!] \;\Rightarrow\; [\![\mathrm{EXP}_1]\!] \subseteq [\![\mathsf{fst}(\mathrm{EXP})]\!]$$

Give the constraint for **snd**. Show that the techniques from Section 5.3 and 5.4 can still be used to find solutions.

14. Use the answer to exercise 5.13 to analyze the following program:

```
class A
   method m(i)
       pair(i, i+1)
   end
end

snd((A new).m(7))
```

15. Show how program transformations can improve the analysis of pairs described in exercise 5.13.
16. Extend the technique from exercise 5.13 to handle broadcasting, as described in exercise 4.17.

6

Inheritance

This chapter discusses different uses for inheritance; argues that not all class hierarchies should be considered well-formed; points out problems related to inheritance of recursive classes; presents an algorithm that resolves inheritance as expansion of code; demonstrates a run-time model that allows reuse of compiled code; and discusses the relationship to the inheritance mechanisms used in existing languages.

6.1   Superclasses and Subclasses

Inheritance plays dual rôles in object-oriented programming: it can be used for conceptual modeling and code reuse. This section briefly reviews the various ways of defining and using inheritance, and as a compromise we decide to study a version where subclasses always are extensions of superclasses.

Inheritance was introduced as a part of the SIMULA language. The main motivation was to allow the program to be structured around the conceptual hierarchies that occur naturally in the simulation domain. Thus, each class should correspond to a *concept*, and the subclasses to *subconcepts*. The entire class hierarchy models a classification hierarchy.

When this methodology is strictly adhered to, it becomes a natural part of the programming process to repeatedly restructure the class hierarchy. Ideally, the class hierarchy should always model the most logical and intellectually satisfying classification of the involved concepts. This reduces code reuse to a secondary, though still important, issue. The SIMULA language encourages the conceptual modeling methodology by disallowing methods from a superclass to be canceled or redefined in subclasses. Also, the inner construct ensures that the superclass code is always executed, forcing a partial preservation of behavior.

Inheritance is viewed differently by proponents of the *rapid prototyping* philosophy that is often associated with languages like SMALLTALK and SELF.

Their emphasis is on code reuse, and inheritance is simply the mechanism by which this is obtained.

The hierarchy of standard classes in SMALLTALK reveals this attitude. The class Dictionary is a subclass of the class Set, even though they are not conceptually related in any convincing manner. In particular, many of the Set methods are missing from Dictionary. The reason is simply that a part of the Set implementation could be grabbed as a basis for the implementation of Dictionary. The superfluous Set methods were then canceled in Dictionary, after which the necessary changes and extensions were performed.

When code reuse is the prime concern, then it seems natural to make the inheritance mechanism liberal in its ability to modify the superclass. In particular, it should be possible to cancel or redefine methods. At its extreme, this means that there need not be any conceptual relation between a superclass and a subclass.

In BOPL we make a compromise between the two attitudes and choose what we will call *monotonic* inheritance. The basic philosophy is that a subclass must be an *extension* of the superclass.

Thus, in a subclass one may add new methods and instance variables. It is also permissible to redefine method *bodies*. In subclasses one can gain access to the old implementation through the meta-variable super.

This choice implies that many properties of the superclass will be preserved in the subclass. In Section 6.3 will shall discuss how further to preserve the *recursive structure* of the subclass. As presented in Section 6.5, our notion of inheritance allows compiled code to be reused. The syntax for BOPL with inheritance is as follows.

```
CLASS     ::=  class ID inherits ID
                VARLIST? METHODLIST?
               end
EXP       ::=  super
```

A class definition may optionally inherit from another. The meta-variable super is equivalent to self, except when it occurs as the receiver in a message send. In this case, it invokes the corresponding method in the superclass. The precise semantics is explained in Section 6.4.

6.2   Well-Formedness

A program that uses inheritance is traditionally thought of as a *tree* of class specifications. In this section we argue that more information can be gained from viewing the program as a *graph* with two kinds of edges. Based on this analysis, we argue for a *well-formedness* criterion for the use of inheritance.

6.2.1 Is-a and Has-a Relations

The class hierarchy is always shaped as a tree or, more properly, as a *forest*, which is a collection of disjoint trees. Typically, it is depicted in the following manner.

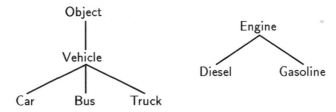

Here, superclasses are on top of subclasses. We can also introduce a binary relation on classes, called **is-a**. It simply states the existence of edges in the forest, such that for example Truck **is-a** Vehicle.

It may seem somewhat redundant to introduce this extra terminology, but we want to refine the analysis by introducing another binary relation, called **has-a**. Intuitively, the relation A **has-a** B holds whenever a B-object is a constituent part of an A-object. For example, is seems reasonable that Vehicle **has-a** Engine. Technically, A **has-a** B holds whenever the implementation of the class A refers to the class B. In untyped BOPL programs, this can only take place in connection with **new** and **instance-of** expressions. In typed BOPL programs, the types may also contain names of classes.

We will depict a collection of classes as a directed graph, called the *class graph*. The nodes are names of classes, and there are two kinds of edges corresponding to **is-a** and **has-a** relations. The former is denoted by solid arrows and the latter by dashed arrows. The following is a possible class graph for the above example.

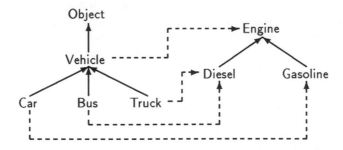

Some structures are immediately seen from such graphs. We say that a class A is *recursive* if A **has-a** A, and that the classes B and C are *mutually* recursive if B **has-a** C and C **has-a** B. As an example, consider the following schematic BOPL program.

```
class U                         class W
    var a: U                        var c: V
end                             end

class V inherits U              class R inherits V
    var b: W                        var d: W
end                             end
```

Its class graph looks as follows.

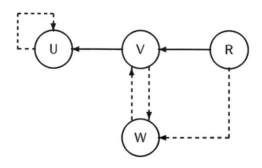

Thus, U is recursive, and V and W are mutually recursive.

6.2.2   Well-Formed Hierarchies

We shall argue that not all programs using inheritance are meaningful. Furthermore, the well-formedness of a program is determined by simple properties of its class graph. Note that since the syntax only allows *single* inheritance, it follows that no class graph derived from a BOPL program can contain a node with two outgoing **is-a** edges. That is, the inheritance hierarchy is always a forest.

The general well-formedness requirement will uphold the principle that a superclass can be compiled independently of all its subclasses. This property is not implied by the syntax itself, but it is easily stated in terms of the class graph: *no directed cycle may contain an is-a edge*. This is a rather abstract phrasing, and in the following we will shall focus on a couple of special cases.

An immediate consequence is that the **is-a** edges cannot form a cycle by themselves. This would happen with the following program, in which two classes inherit each other.

```
class X inherits Y
    method m() returns Int
        0
    end
end

class Y inherits X
    method m() returns Int
        1
    end
end
```

A further problem with mutual inheritance is that we now have two methods named m that each attempts to redefine the other. So which one should win? There is no apparent basis for making this decision.

The independence principle also disallows situations like the following.

```
class X
    var a: Y
end

class Y inherits X
    method m() returns Int
        1
    end
end
```

Here, we have a cycle consisting of the **is-a** edge from Y to X and the **has-a** edge from X to Y. Thus, this class hierarchy is not well-formed. We must reject it, because the class X cannot be compiled independently of Y. We must know about Y in order to type check X.

The only cycles we allow are the ones that originate from mutual *recursion*, which is exemplified by the following program.

```
class X
    var a: Y
end

class Y
    var b: X
end
```

In this case, the class graph contains a cycle consisting of a **has-a** edge from X to Y and a **has-a** edge from Y to X. Since no **is-a** edge is involved, the class hierarchy is well-formed. Of course, the two classes must be compiled as a group.

Note that only *directed* cycles with **is-a** edges are forbidden. The following program contains an undirected cycle but is well-formed.

```
class X
    var a: Int
end

class Y inherits ⌷X⌷
    var b: ⌷X⌷
end
```

Here, Y inherits X and also introduces an instance variable of type X. Neither prohibits the separate compilation of X.

For larger programs with more complex class graphs the general requirement must be applied. As for these above small examples, the deeper meaning is to ensure that a superclass can be compiled independently of its subclasses. Note that both the example programs in the previous section are well-formed.

6.3   Capture of Recursion

Inheritance is sometimes thought of as a simple *cut-and-paste* operation on source code. This is too simplistic in connection with recursive classes, since the recursive structure of the superclass is then not captured in the subclass. Instead, we propose a technique that remedies this shortcoming.

6.3.1   Most Classes are Recursive

Most classes in object-oriented programs are recursive. For example, consider the following class of simple lists.

```
class List
    var head: Int; tail: ⌷List⌷
    method Set(h: Int; t: ⌷List⌷) returns ⌷List⌷
        head := h; tail := t; self
    end
    method Cons(h: Int) returns ⌷List⌷
        (self class new).Set(h, self)
    end
    method Car() returns Int
        head
    end
```

```
        method Cdr() returns  List
            tail
        end
    end
```

A typical value can be sketched as follows.

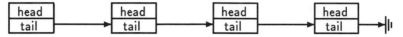

This example shows some of the many ways in which classes may refer to themselves.

- The class can define recursive structures through the declaration of instance variables such as tail: List.
- The tradition of returning self from methods, as it happens in e.g. Set, makes the return type a recursive reference.
- Data type operations, like Cdr, will often have instances of the class as arguments or return values.

Thus, the recursive structure of a class is an important characteristic. We contend that it should be preserved in subclasses.

6.3.2   What is the Type of Self?

Consider a subclass of the List class. It extends the superclass by introducing an instance variable that notes the length of the list.

```
        class LList inherits List
            var length: Int
            method Length() returns Int
                length
            end
        end
```

We surely need to make further modifications to maintain the correct length information, but already now we have some important questions to ask about the type of self in this subclass. For example, is the instance variable tail of type List or of type LList? If inheritance is viewed as simply cut-and-paste of source code, then LList is equivalent to the following implementation.

```
        class LList
            var head: Int; tail:  List
            var length: Int
```

```
    method Set(h: Int; t: List ) returns List
        head := h; tail := t; self
    end
    method Cons(h: Int) returns List
        (self class new).Set(h, self)
    end
    method Car() returns Int
        head
    end
    method Cdr() returns List
        tail
    end
    method Length() returns Int
        length
    end
end
```

A typical value now looks as follows.

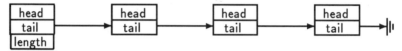

But this was not what we intended! For example, the class defines lists in which only the first element has a **length** component. Also, the class is not statically correct, since the body of **Set** returns an **LList** where a **List** is required. This type error cannot even be fixed with a dynamic type check.

In languages that use class types, the situation would be different if we used the cone set ↑List everywhere in place of List. In this case, the subclass would be equivalent to the following implementation, since ↑List expands to the set {List,LList} under the closed-world assumption.

```
class LList
    var head: Int; tail: {List,LList}
    var length: Int
    method Set(h: Int; t: {List,LList} ) returns {List,LList}
        head := h; tail := t; self
    end
    method Cons(h: Int) returns {List,LList}
        (self class new).Set(h, self)
    end
    method Car() returns Int
        head
    end
```

```
            method Cdr() returns  {List,LList}
                tail
            end
            method Length() returns Int
                length
            end
        end
```

The following is now a typical value.

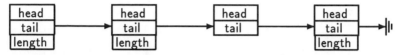

This class is statically correct, but it has other problems. To begin with, it defines lists in which it is optional whether elements have length components. It cannot be guaranteed that *all* elements are instances of LList. This gives a lot of slack that causes problems for applications. For example, the innocent looking expression:

$$(\textsf{LList new}).\textsf{Cons}(17).\textsf{Cons}(18).\textsf{Length}()$$

is rejected by the type checker, because the Length message cannot be guaranteed to be understood. Similarly, if L is a variable of type LList, then the expression:

$$\textsf{L} := \textsf{L.Cdr}()$$

will by the type checker be transformed into:

$$\textsf{L} := (\textsf{L.Cdr() instance-of LList})$$

in which a—probably superfluous—dynamic check has been inserted. Such anomalies can be found in many realistic situations. The class that we most likely wanted to specify is the following.

```
        class LList
            var head: Int; tail: LList
            var length: Int
            method Set(h: Int; t: LList ) returns LList
                head := h; tail := t; self
            end
            method Cons(h: Int) returns LList
                (self class new).Set(h, self)
            end
```

```
    method Car() returns Int
        head
    end
    method Cdr() returns  LList
        tail
    end
    method Length() returns Int
        length
    end
end
```

A typical value looks as follows.

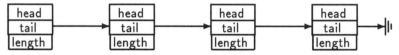

Here, all elements are guaranteed to have length components. Furthermore, all the type errors that haunted the previous definitions will not occur. We shall say that the recursive structure of the superclass has been *captured* by the subclass.

In BOPL, inheritance will by default perform such capture. It could be argued that it should be optional for the programmer whether this happens. One idea is to allow the keyword **selfclass** as a token in the types. It would simply be a synonym for the name of the surrounding class, but during inheritance it would signify capture of the corresponding occurrence of recursion.

There are two objections to this idea, however. First, as the following section will show, it can only be used for the simplest recursive classes. Second, if capture is not wanted, then maybe the program could be written in a different way. Consider the situation where we actually wanted lists in which only the first element had a **length** component. In this case, we are really forming a *pair* consisting of a list and an integer. Hence, the program should look something like the following.

```
    class Pair
        var list: List
        var length: Int

        . . .
    end
```

The use of inheritance in this situation corresponds to a confusion of the **is-a** and **has-a** relations, which is also at the root of many anomalies found in the SMALLTALK standard class hierarchy.

It might be believed that capture of recursion makes the reuse of compiled code difficult or even impossible. After all, some types in the superclass

implementation must be changed. This is not the case, however. In Section
6.5 we present a simple implementation technique that handles this apparent
problem.

6.3.3   Mutually Recursive Classes

Recursive classes are commonplace, and so are *mutually* recursive ones. Many
data structures are most conveniently expressed in this manner. A canonical
example is the representation of parse trees for all but the simplest context-
free grammars.

   In the following, we shall use small grammars as examples. They will be
the minimal ones illustrating our ideas. For a more realistic example, one may
think of parse trees for the context-free syntax of the BOPL language itself.

   Consider the following simple grammar.

$$X \quad ::= \quad (\text{INT}) \, X \mid \varepsilon$$

Its parse trees could be represented by the following class.

```
class X
    var i: Int
    var x: X
end
```

Suppose now that we want to add some further information of type T to
each object. If we think of a compilation process, then parse tree nodes are
gradually enriched with symbol and type information in subsequent passes. A
straightforward solution is to define:

```
class XX inherits X
    var t: T
end
```

Without capture, only the first node will contain the extra information of type
T; with capture, all node do. In this simple case, it would be possible to use
the selfclass token and define:

```
class X
    var i: Int
    var x: selfclass
end

class XX inherits X
    var t: T
end
```

which would yield the desired result. Consider next the following grammar.

$$X \quad ::= \quad (\text{INT})\ Y \ | \ \varepsilon$$
$$Y \quad ::= \quad (\text{BOOL})\ X \ | \ \varepsilon$$

Again, the corresponding parse trees are easily defined as follows.

    class X
        var i: Int
        var y: $\boxed{\text{Y}}$
    end

    class Y
        var b: Bool
        var x: $\boxed{\text{X}}$
    end

As before, the nodes with integer components must be extended with some extra information of type T. The simplistic inheritance without capture fails again, and now even the **selfclass** idea cannot help. It is simply wrong to use it in either of the y: Y or x: X declarations.

The only satisfactory solution is to require that the inheritance mechanism *always* captures the *entire* recursive structure of the superclass. Thus, the definition:

    class XX **inherits** X
        var t: T
    end

must yield *two* new classes. One is the XX class itself, and the other is a YY class with which XX can be mutually recursive. That is, the result should be equivalent to the following.

    class XX
        var i: Int
        var t: T
        var y: $\boxed{\text{YY}}$
    end

    class YY
        var b: Bool
        var x: $\boxed{\text{XX}}$
    end

It may not seem obvious that these relations can be detected in every case or that code reuse can be realized. However, affirmative answers to these questions will be given in Sections 6.4 and 6.5. A more complicated hierarchy is the following first shown in Section 6.2.1.

class U   **class** W
    var a: U   **var** c: V
end   **end**

class V **inherits** U   **class** R **inherits** V
    var b: W   **var** d: W
end   **end**

With full capture, it will be equivalent to these definitions.

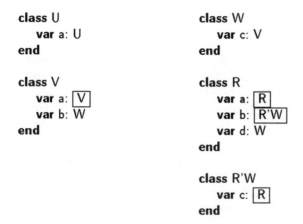

class U   **class** W
    var a: U   **var** c: V
end   **end**

class V   **class** R
    var a: $\boxed{\text{V}}$ **var** a: $\boxed{\text{R}}$
    var b: W   **var** b: $\boxed{\text{R'W}}$
end   **var** d: W
                                                     end

                                                     class R'W
                                                         var c: $\boxed{\text{R}}$
                                                     end

Note that the class R'W has been introduced as a recursive companion to R. Also, the recursion through the a-component is captured in the classes V and R. The new class graph, which is of course without is-a edges, looks as follows.

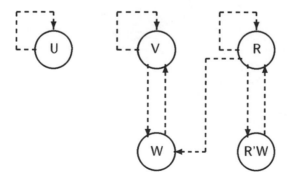

In conclusion, we believe that capture of recursion is an essential feature of inheritance; furthermore, this cannot be emulated with the introduction of a selfclass token.

6.3.4   Avoiding Capture

In some cases, we do not want all recursive occurrences to be captured. We can achieve this by allowing multiple tokens for the same class. We extend the BOPL grammar as follows.

$$\text{CLASS} \quad ::= \quad \textbf{class } \text{ID}_1 \textbf{ renews } \text{ID}_2$$

This defines ID_1 as a new token for the class ID_2. There is a subtle relationship between these multiple tokens. With respect to the type rules they are different. Thus, with the definitions:

class Y **renews** X
class Z **renews** X

all of the sets $\{X\}$, $\{X,Y\}$, $\{X,Z\}$, and $\{X,Y,Z\}$ are different. However, all these tokens denote the *same* class. Thus, X, Y, and Z have the same super- and subclasses. This can be illustrated with the following class hierarchy.

When X is renewed as Y and Z, then we get the following "token hierarchy".

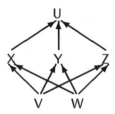

Of course, we do *not* have multiple inheritance—the classes X, Y, and Z all have identical implementations.

This mechanism will prove useful in Chapter 7, and it certainly allows us to avoid unwanted capture. As an example, consider the following class hierarchy.

class C **renews** A

class A
   var x: A
     var y: $\boxed{\text{C}}$
end

```
class B inherits A
    var z: Int
end
```

It expands into these classes.

```
class C renews A
```

```
class A
    var x: A
    var y: C
end
```

```
class B
    var x: B
    var y: C
    var z: Int
end
```

A language designer has in total four options:

1) capture never happens;
2) capture does not happen by default, but it can be explicitly requested;
3) capture happens by default, but it can be explicitly avoided; or
4) capture always happens.

Of these, we believe that 1) is the worst choice since capture is often useful; 2) is better, but insufficient for mutual recursion; 4) is useful also for mutual recursion; and 3) is the most general option, which is realized through our inheritance definition combined with class renewal.

6.4   The Inheritance Expansion Algorithm

The previous section explained several instances of inheritance by showing *expanded* versions of the subclasses. In this section, we shall discuss how *every* instance of inheritance can be similarly explained.

6.4.1   Expanding Source Code

A naïve understanding of inheritance is as a cut-and-paste mechanism. The source code from the superclass is copied into the subclass, as indicated by the following picture.

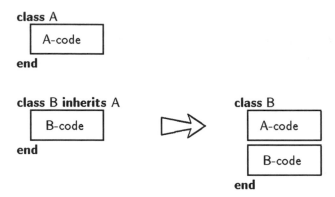

We shall basically follow this idea, except that several refinements are necessary in order to take proper care of **super**, redefinitions, and recursive capture.

The expansion approach is well-suited for explaining the semantics of inheritance. However, it is a poor implementation strategy, since it only allows reuse of source code rather than compiled code. In Section 6.5 we demonstrate how our brand of inheritance can be implemented with the full exploitation of the reuse potential.

It is worth considering how large a program can become after expansion of inheritance. This can be estimated by looking at the simple cut-and-paste mechanism. It is a folklore result that a quadratic blowup in size can be achieved, for example by the following classes.

```
class C₁
    var x₁: Int
end

class C₂ inherits C₁
    var x₂: Int
end

class C₃ inherits C₂
    var x₃: Int
end
    ⋮
class Cₙ inherits Cₙ₋₁
    var xₙ: Int
end
```

It is more subtle to see that the above is the worst case, so we shall take the small effort to show this. The problem can be simply modeled as follows.

Consider a finite tree in which each node is labeled with a string over some alphabet. This corresponds to our inheritance hierarchy, with the strings being the source code. For such a tree we define its size to be the total length of the strings it contains. The expansion of a tree is obtained by prefixing the string from the root to the strings in the roots of each immediate subtree, and then recursively expanding these subtrees. This is shown in the following illustration.

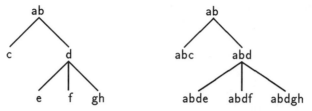

The question is now, how much larger can the expansion become? We can transform a tree into a *normal form* of the same size, in which each string has length one. This is done by an easy transformation sketched below.

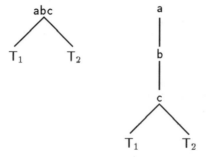

Clearly, the size of the expansion is bigger for the normal form than for the original tree. Thus, it is sufficient to find an upper bound for normal trees. We introduce the notation $W(n)$ to denote the largest size of the expansion of any normal tree with n nodes. It is easy to see that $W(n) + W(m) \leq W(n+m)$, since the worst-case tree with n nodes can adopt the worst-case tree with m nodes as a subtree and form a single tree with $n+m$ nodes whose expansion is larger than $W(n) + W(m)$, but of course at most $W(n+m)$. We can now set up the following inequality.

$$
\begin{aligned}
W(0) &= 0 \\
W(n) &\leq (n-1) + 1 + \max\{\Sigma_i W(k_i) \mid \Sigma_i k_i = n - 1\} \\
&\leq n + W(n-1)
\end{aligned}
$$

This holds, since the expansion of a normal tree can be obtained by first expanding the subtrees and then prefixing the root letter to the $(n-1)$ nodes in the subtrees. Solving the corresponding equality, we get the desired upper bound of $W(n) \in O(n^2)$. Thus, expanding inheritance can cause a worst-case quadratic increase in the size of a program.

6.4.2   Handling Super

Some obvious problems with the cut-and-paste semantics relate to **super** and the redefinition of methods. The ordinary BOPL language does not support the meta-variable **super**, nor does it allow more than one implementation of a given method. This answer is to follow these simple rules, when pasting code from a superclass to a subclass.

- If a method is being redefined, the name of the superclass is appended to the name of the method.
- If **super** occurs as receiver of a message, then the name of the superclass is appended to the message.
- All occurrences of **super** are replaced by **self**.

The application of these rules can be illustrated by the following untyped program, in which a collection of geometrical objects is sketched.

```
class Geometrical
    var x, y
    method Set(x0, y0)
        x := x0;  y := y0;  self
    end
end

class Rectangle inherits Geometrical
    var l, w
    method Base(l0, w0)
        l := l0;  w := w0;  self
    end
    method Area()
        l*w
    end
    method Scale(s)
        l := l*s;  w := w*s;  self
    end
end

class Box inherits Rectangle
    var h
```

```
            method Height(h0)
               h := h0
            end
            method Volume()
               self.Area()*h
            end
            method Scale(s)
               super.Scale(s) ; h := h*s; self
            end
         end
```

```
      (Box new).Set(0, 0).Base(3, 4).Height(5).Scale(2).Volume()
```

The result is of course 480. After expansion of inheritance, the program looks as follows.

```
      class Geometrical
         var x, y
         method Set(x0, y0)
            x := x0; y := y0; self
         end
      end
```

```
      class Rectangle
         var x, y , l, w
         method Set (x0, y0)
            x := x0; y := y0; self
         end
         method Base(l0, w0)
            l := l0; w := w0; self
         end
         method Area()
            l*w
         end
         method Scale(s)
            l := l*s; w := w*s; self
         end
      end
```

```
      class Box
         var x, y, l, w , h
         method Set (x0, y0)
            x := x0; y := y0; self
         end
```

```
method  Base (l0, w0)
    l := l0;  w := w0;  self
end
method  Area ()
    l*w
end
method  Scale$Rectangle (s)
    l := l*s;  w := w*s;  self
end
method Height(h0)
    h := h0
end
method Volume()
    self.Area()*h
end
method Scale(s)
    self . Scale$Rectangle (s);  h := h*s;  self
end
end
```

(Box **new**).Set(0, 0).Base(3, 4).Height(5).Scale(2).Volume()

To ensure unique names, a $-symbol is used in the renaming of methods. Note that two different versions of Scale exist in the class Box.

6.4.3   Handling Capture

The technique described above does not handle capture of recursion, which sometimes requires that we introduce more classes. In a previous example, we have seen how a hierarchy of four classes can expand into five individual classes.

To do this correctly, we must process the classes one at a time in a particular order. We define the relation X≤Y on classes to hold if X=Y or there is a path from Y to X containing at least one **is-a** edge. Because of well-formedness, this is a partial order. We shall process the classes *topologically* sorted according to ≤. The following is from left to right a possible topological order of a class graph.

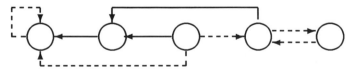

The classes will be expanded from left to right in the topological order. At any given stage, an initial segment has been processed and does not have any outgoing is-a edges.

We can now give the expansion algorithm. It relies on a simple procedure SUBST(f,C), where f is a partial function on class names and C is a class. The result is a copy of the implementation of C, in which class names have been substituted according to f; if a class name is not in the domain of f, then it is not changed.

```
let v₁, v₂, ..., vₙ be a topological sorting of the nodes;
for i := 1 to n do
    if vᵢ is-a w then
        H := {u | w has-a* u} \ {w};
        f := {w ↦ vᵢ} ∪ {u ↦ v'ᵢu | u ∈ H};
        for u ∈ H do
            vᵢ'u := SUBST(f,u)
        end;
        cut-and-paste from SUBST(f,w) to vᵢ
    end
end
```

Each class is processed in turn. If it does not inherit, then nothing further happens; otherwise, a set of recursive companions is computed by following has-a edges from the parent. They are then suitably renamed, and finally a cut-and-paste is performed as described in Section 6.4.2.

A small example will illustrate the workings of this algorithm. We now show in detail, how the following familiar hierarchy is expanded.

```
class U                          class W
    var a: U                         var c: V
end                              end


class V inherits U               class R inherits V
    var b: W                         var d: W
end                              end
```

A valid topological order is as follows.

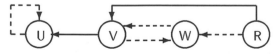

- First, U is processed. Since it does not inherit, nothing happens.
- Then V is up. The parent U has only **has-a** edges to itself, so we simply cut-and-paste from U and replace references to U by references to V.
- We move on to W. It does not inherit, so it is already processed.

- Finally, we come to R. It inherits from V which has a **has-a** edge to the processed class W. Hence, we create a copy named R'W. Then we cut-and-paste code from V to R. We complete the process by going through R and R'W, replacing references to V by references to R and prefixing occurrences of W with R.

We obtain the expected expansion. The result is, of course, independent of the chosen topological order.

As a final example, consider the following sketch of a typed version of the geometrical classes.

```
class Geometrical
    var x, y: Int
    method Set(x0, y0: Int) returns Geometrical
end

class Rectangle inherits Geometrical
    var l, w: Int
    method Base(l0, w0: Int) returns Rectangle
    method Area() returns Int
    method Scale(s: Int) returns Rectangle
end

class Box inherits Rectangle
    var h: Int
    method Height(l0, w0, h0: Int) returns Box
    method Volume() returns Int
    method Scale(s: Int) returns Box
end
```

After expansion with capture, the method headers look as follows.

```
class Geometrical
    var x, y: Int
    method Set(x0, y0: Int) returns Geometrical
end

class Rectangle
    var x, y, l, w: Int
    method Set(x0, y0: Int) returns  Rectangle
    method Base(l0, w0: Int) returns Rectangle
    method Area() returns Int
    method Scale(s: Int) returns Rectangle
end
```

```
class Box
    var x, y, l, w, h: Int
    method Set(x0, y0: Int) returns  Box
    method Base(l0, w0: Int) returns  Box
    method Area() returns Int
    method Scale$Rectangle(l0, w0: Int) returns  Box
    method Height(h0: Int) returns Box
    method Volume() returns Int
    method Scale(s: Int) returns Box
end
```

6.4.4   Type Correctness of Subclasses

We now demonstrate that if the superclass is statically type correct, then so is the inherited part of a subclass.

After expansion of inheritance we can construct an *exploded* class graph which reveals important structures. As usual, the nodes correspond to the existing classes. The edges, however, are different. A solid edge from B to A indicates that B has been constructed as a subclass of A. We extend this relationship to include that B may be constructed as a modified copy of A during the expansion. The dashed edges still indicate **has-a** relations, but if a class C has n references to classes in its implementation, then it will have n outgoing dashed edges labeled $1, 2, \ldots, n$. In other words, the following edge:

will be seen whenever D is the textually i'th occurrence of a class name in the expanded implementation of C. The exploded class graph for our small running example looks as follows.

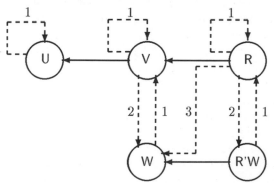

After expansion of inheritance, the exploded class graph satisfies the following two conditions which we combined shall denote *consistency*.

a) Whenever the edges on the left exist, then so do the ones on the right.

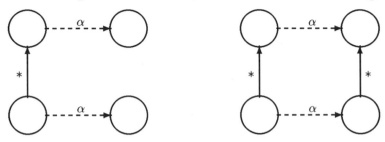

In other words, classes can only be replaced by subclasses. Here, the *
indicates zero or more solid edges, i.e., the reflexive and transitive closure
of the **is-a** relation; α indicates a path of labeled **has-a** edges.

b) Whenever the edges on the left exist, then so do the ones on the right.

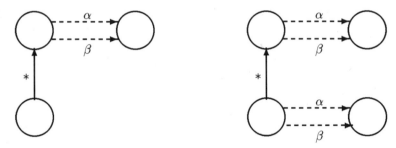

In other words, pairs of equal classes can only be replaced by other pairs
of equal classes. Here, α and β indicate possibly different paths of labeled
has-a edges.

It should be fairly clear that expansion of inheritance leads to consistency. If
we followed the naïve cut-and-paste strategy, then it would trivially hold. The
renamings of methods and messages performed to give the correct semantics
of **super** does not change names of classes. Capture of recursion evidently
does change class names. However, a class is always substituted by a subclass,
which satifies condition a), and this substitution is determined by a function,
which satifies condition b).

Consistency implies the important property that when types are finite sets
of classes, then the inherited part of a subclass need never be type checked
again. This is caused by conditions a) and b), which exactly guarantee that the
veracity of the type constraints remain unchanged. Given that Int and Bool
tokens cannot be replaced, only a few of the constraints from Section 4.3.3
need to be reviewed. Most set inclusions will not change, since on both sides
we apply the *same* function from tokens to tokens. That is, if the inclusion:

$$\{A,B,C\} \subseteq \{A,B,C,D,E\}$$

holds and f is a substitution function, then so will:

$$\{f(A),f(B),f(C)\} \subseteq \{f(A),f(B),f(C),f(D),f(E)\}$$

The only complications are safety constraints of the form:

$$X \subseteq \{all\ classes\}$$
$$X \subseteq \{all\ legal\ receiver\ classes\}$$

Because of condition a), however, both of these will also remain unchanged. The novel part of a subclass must of course be type checked on its own.

Note that we have extended the notion of subclassing to go beyond merely inheritance. A modified copy created during capture is also considered to be a subclass of the original. This idea will be substantiated further in the following section as well as in Chapter 7.

6.5   The Run-Time Model for Inheritance

The semantics of inheritance has been explained as expansion of source code. This seems to suggest that code inherited in subclasses must be recompiled. In this section we demonstrate how to reuse compiled code and still handle method redefinitions and recursive capture.

6.5.1   Reuse of Compiled Code

The implementation of plain BOPL presented in Chapter 3 was basically an interpreter. Now, we must explain how to *compile* code, in order to set the ground rules for evaluating code reuse.

We will still have an explicit representation of the class library but it will no longer be simply as text. The bodies of methods will be compiled in the traditional sense. In order to invoke a method implementation, one must push the arguments onto the run-time stack and perform a call to an appropriate code address. For the language without inheritance, the state from Section 3.2 will now look as follows.

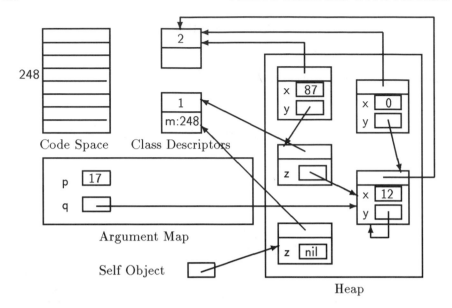

All the methods are compiled and placed in the code space. Each class is described by a record, which contains its number of instance variables and a start address for each method name. To describe the generated code, we need a few macro definitions.

- size(C) denotes for a class C its number of instance variables.
- method(C,m) denotes the start address of the method named m or ? if this is not defined.
- class(x) denotes the class descriptor of the object x, which it contains a pointer to.
- allocate(C) yields a pointer to a new object of class C with size(C) instance variables, all initialized to nil.
- self denotes the self object in the current state.

When regarding code reuse, only three kinds of expressions are interesting. They are message sends, **new**, and **instance-of**. We shall explain how to generate code for each of these.

- The message send $x.m(a_1, a_2, \ldots, a_n)$ generates the code:

```
push x
push a₁
push a₂
  ⋮
push aₙ
call M-lookup(class(x),m)
```

where M-lookup is defined as:

$$\text{M-lookup}(C,m) = \begin{cases} \text{message-not-understood} & \text{if method}(C,m)=? \\ \text{method}(C,m) & \text{otherwise} \end{cases}$$

- The expression A **new** generates the code:

  push allocate(A)

- The expression x **instance-of** A generates the code:

  if class(x)$\neq$A then run-time-error

which can of course be generalized to larger sets.

Code reuse requires that we do not *modify* the code space—it can only be extended.

6.5.2 Dynamic Lookup

When inheritance is introduced, then we extend the class descriptors with another field containing a pointer to the class descriptor for the superclass or nil if no such exists. We need some more macro definitions.

- super(C) denotes the pointer to the superclass descriptor of C.
- size(C) counts the total number of instance variables in a class, even those introduced in superclasses.

Redefinitions of methods are, of course, handled by *method lookup*. We change the definition of M-lookup as follows.

$$\text{M-lookup}(C,m) = \begin{cases} \text{message-not-understood} & \text{if } C=\text{nil} \\ \text{method}(C,m) & \text{if method}(C,m)\neq? \\ \text{M-lookup}(\text{super}(C),m) & \text{otherwise} \end{cases}$$

Thus, the search for an implementation of a method happens bottom-up through the class hierarchy. If the method m has been redefined, then the code for the message send **super.m**(a_1,a_2,...,a_n) is:

```
push self
push a1
push a2
⋮
push an
call M-lookup(super(class(x)),m)
```

The capture of simple recursion can be easily handled by replacing all recursive references to the class by class(self). General capture is more complicated and requires a technique similar to method lookup.

In the generated code, classes only occur in **new** and **instance-of** expressions. Instead of hard-wiring them into the code, we shall introduce the concept of *instantiators*, which can be thought of as the names of pseudo-methods that return classes.

We extend class descriptors to include a mapping from instantiators to classes and introduce a final macro.

- instantiator(C,w) denotes the class associated with w in C or ? if no such exists.

A general class descriptor now looks as follows.

super
size
methods
instantiators

The code for the expression A **new** is changed to:

$$\text{push allocate(I-lookup(class(self),w))}$$

if w is the instantiator that maps to A. A similar change is performed in the code for **instance-of**. The idea is now to allow *redefinition* of instantiators, such that we define:

$$\text{I-lookup}(C,w) = \begin{cases} \text{instantiator}(C,w) & \text{if instantiator}(C,w) \neq ? \\ \text{I-lookup}(\text{super}(C),w) & \text{otherwise} \end{cases}$$

When a class is copied as a recursive companion to a subclass, then the copy becomes a subclass of the original. By looking at the class descriptor of the original, the compiler can compute an appropriate redefining instantiator map.

This is best illustrated by an example. Consider the following untyped class hierarchy.

```
class A                          class C inherits A
  var x                            method m()
  method m()                         A new
    B new                          end
  end                            end
end

class B
  var y, z
  method n()
    A new
  end
end
```

It expands into these classes.

```
class A                          class C
  var x                            var x
  method m()                       method m$A()
    B new                            C'B new
  end                              end
end                                method m()
                                     A new
class B                            end
  var y, z                       end
  method n()
    A new                        class C'B
  end                              var y, z
end                                method n()
                                     C new
                                   end
                                 end
```

At runtime, the code space looks as follows.

```
248: push allocate(I-lookup(class(self),w_1))
     return
  .
  .
  .
319: push allocate(I-lookup(class(self),w_2))
     return
  .
  .
  .
387: push allocate(I-lookup(class(self),w_3))
     return
```

It goes together with these four class descriptors.

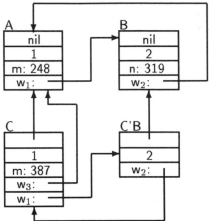

It can be easily verified that the run-time behavior will be the same as that for the expanded class hierarchy. Note that we have three method implementations that are used for five methods—a tangible indication of code reuse.

6.6   Class Types

This section briefly reviews the inheritance mechanisms of the languages SIMULA, SMALLTALK, C++, and EIFFEL with the emphasis on monotonicity, well-formedness, and capture.

SIMULA features monotonic inheritance and the inner statement encourages behavioral consistency. It supports just single inheritance without cycles. Capture of recursion is not supported, but in the BETA language it can be programmed using virtual patterns.

SMALLTALK basically features single, monotonic inheritance without cycles. However, a method can be canceled in a subclass by being redefined to provoke a message-not-understood error. This facility encourages the less disciplined approach to code reuse. Capture is not possible.

The inheritance mechanism in C++ is monotonic without cycles, and multiple inheritance is allowed in situations where name conflicts do not arise. Again, capture is not supported.

EIFFEL features a liberal notion of inheritance. The multiple superclasses can be modified in every imaginable way, and there is an intricate scheme for resolving name conflicts through renamings. Cycles are not allowed. Capture of single recursion is possible: the type like Current plays the rôle of selfclass.

Bibliographical Notes

For an overview of how to use inheritance for conceptual modeling, see the paper by Knudsen and Madsen [36]. Various other ways of using and classifying inheritance mechanisms have been discussed by Wegner and Zdonik [72] and Halbert and O'Brian [29]. Cook [18] analyzed the use of inheritance in the SMALLTALK class library. For a discussion of the differences between self and inner, see the paper by Bracha and Cook [6].

Our well-formedness criterion for class graphs has much in common with the "Cycle-free alternation axiom" of Bergstein and Lieberherr [39].

The need for capturing recursion has been discussed by Meyer [45], Cook, Hill, and Canning [14], Hur and Chon [33], and Sakkinen [60], among others. The idea of letting capture be the default and then provide explicit syntax for avoiding it was suggested by us [54].

Inheritance can be given a compositional semantics, as demonstrated by Cook and the first author [15, 16], Reddy [59], Kamin [35], and Hense [31]. The first of these papers proved that the given semantics is equivalent to the operational explanation given by Goldberg and Robson [26].

Our run-time model is an extension of one we used in [56].

Exercises

1. Draw the class graph for the geometry classes from Section 6.4.2.
2. Which of the following class graphs are well-formed?

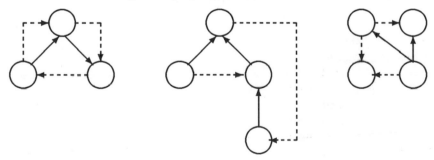

3. Suppose a tree in normal form from Section 6.4.1 is perfectly balanced. What is then the size of its expansion?
4. Change BOPL to use inner rather than super. Show, in analogy with Section 6.4.2, how to expand this construct.
5. Suppose BOPL did not capture class recursion but allowed the use of selfclass. Consider then the following program.

```
class Point
    var x, y: Int
    method Set(xs, ys: Int) returns Point
        x := xs;
        y := ys;
        self
    end
    method Move(dx, dy: Int) returns Point
        self.Set(x+dx, y+dy)
    end
end

class ColorPoint inherits Point
    var color: Int
    method SetColor(x: Int) returns Int
        color := c
    end
end

(ColorPoint new).Move(2, 3).SetColor(200)
```

a) Why is this program not statically type correct?

b) Modify the program using selfclass to make it statically type correct.

6. Expand the following class hierarchy.

```
class A
    var x
    method m()
        A new
    end
    method n()
        A new
    end
end

class B inherits A
    var y
    method m()
        super.m()
    end
end
```

```
class C inherits B
  method m()
    super.m()
  end
  method n()
    super.n()
  end
end
```

7. Show the run-time representation of the class hierarchy from exercise 6.6.
8. Extend the BOPL syntax with:

DEC   ::=   IDLIST : **static** TYPE

A static declaration can never be changed, not even in subclasses. Explain
the further restrictions on consistency of exploded class graphs that must
be imposed to respect static **has-a** edges. Show how this feature can be
used to avoid some cases of method lookup at run-time.

9. Check that the two class graphs in Section 6.2.1 are well-formed.
10. Draw the class graph for the following program.

```
class A
  var x: E
end

class B
  var y: C
end

class C
  var z: A
end

class D inherits A
  method m()
    B new
  end
end

class E inherits C
  method n()
    D new
  end
end
```

Is it well-formed?

11. Consider the following method template.

```
method m(x: S) returns T
   E
end
```

Transform it into an untyped version, where the method body checks at run-time that the types of the argument and the result are as specified. Suppose this transformation is applied to all methods in a program. Does this transformation preserve the class graph? Why?

12. Consider the following class.

```
class Tree
   var l, r: Tree
   var leaf: Bool
   method SetLeaf() returns Tree
      leaf := true; self
   end
   method Set(s, t: Tree) returns Tree
      l := s; r := t; leaf := false; self
   end
   method JoinRight(t: Tree) returns Tree
      (self class new).Set(self, t)
   end
   method Left() returns Tree
      l
   end
   method Right() returns Tree
      r
   end
end
```

Sketch a typical instance of this class (like in Section 6.3.1). Consider the following subclass of the Tree class. It extends the superclass by introducing an instance variable of type integer.

```
class STree inherits Tree
   var c: Int
   method Sum() returns Int
      if leaf then
         c
      else
         self.Left().Sum()+self.Right().Sum()+c
      end
   end
end
```

Suppose that recursion is not captured. Give a definition of **Stree** that does not use inheritance and sketch a typical instance of it. Is the method **Set** statically type correct?

Suppose that we replace by ↑S Tree all occurrences of TREE inside the class **Tree**. Under the closed-world assumption, ↑S Tree expands to the set {Tree,S Tree}. Sketch a typical instance of S Tree under these assumptions. Is the following expression then statically type correct?

$$(STree\ \mathbf{new}).JoinRight((STree\ \mathbf{new}).SetLeaf()).Right().Sum()$$

If recursion is captured, is the expression then statically type correct?

13. Consider the following two classes.

```
class Even
    var eventail: Odd
    method Tail() returns Odd
        eventail
    end
end

class Odd
    var oddtail: Even
    method Tail() returns Even
        oddtail
    end
end
```

The idea is that an instance of for example **Even** may be understood as an alternating list of **Evens** and **Odds**. Draw a typical such instance. Write a new subclass **ColorEven** of **Even** which adds an instance variable color to the even components, all the way down such an alternating list. Write an expression which is statically type correct if recursion is captured, but incorrect if not.

14. Recall the function W from Section 6.4.1.

$$
\begin{aligned}
W(0) &= 0 \\
W(n) &\leq n + W(n-1)
\end{aligned}
$$

Prove by induction that $W(n) \leq n^2$.

15. Show in detail the expansion of the following class hierarchy.

```
class P
    var x: Q
end
```

```
class Q
   var y: R
end

class R
   var z: P
end

class S inherits P
   var v: Q
end
```

16. In Section 6.3.3 is shown the result of expanding the classes U, V, W, and
    R. What would be the result if the classes were expanded without capture
    of recursion?

    Insert some methods and a main expression into the program such that

    a) If the program is expanded *with* capture of recursion, then it is statically
       type correct.
    b) If the program is expanded *without* capture of recursion, then it is *not*
       statically type correct.

7

Genericity

This chapter motivates the idea of genericity; assesses several previous approaches to genericity; introduces the genericity mechanism of "class substitution"; explains the advantages of class substitution compared to other mechanisms; presents an algorithm that resolves class substitution as expansion of code; and discusses the relationship of class substitution to type systems based on class types.

7.1   Why Genericity?

The basic idea of genericity is "substitution of type annotations". This section explains why this is significant.

7.1.1   Substitution of Type Annotations

Consider the following class:

```
class C
    var x, y: T
    method m() returns T
        x := y
    end
end

(C new).m()
```

This class is clearly statically type correct. The key observation is that we can substitute T by any other type and still get a type correct class.

If we want such a slightly different class, then we might of course duplicate the code of the class C and change its type annotations. Such code duplication would be contrary to the code reuse maxim of object-oriented programming, however. It would be better to have a language mechanism that enables us to construct a new class by modifying the type annotations in an existing class. For example, if we want T to be replaced by S, then it should be sufficient to write something like:

> We want a new class D which should be like C, except that all occurrences of T should be replaced by S.

A *genericity* mechanism is what enables us to do this. It offers different possibilities for modifying classes than those provided by inheritance. Genericity and inheritance both construct a new class from an existing class and they differ as follows.

- **Genericity.** Substitution of type annotations.
- **Inheritance.** Addition of variables and methods, and replacement of method bodies.

The two ways of constructing new classes change different parts of a class. Consider for example the class C above. Genericity can change the two type annotations, but not for example the body of the method m. Inheritance, in contrast, can indeed change the body of m, but it cannot change the type annotations.

Recalling that types are invariants, we can restate the comparison of genericity and inheritance.

- **Genericity.** The new class yields the *same behavior* but *new invariants* for that behavior.
- **Inheritance.** The new class yields *new behavior* but with the *same invariants*.

Genericity is intimately connected to static type checking. In the example above, genericity was used to obtain a new statically type correct class from the existing statically type correct class C. This indicates how genericity can be practical: once we have put our hands on a statically type correct class, genericity should enable us to easily obtain new statically type correct classes. This yields a major practical requirement for genericity mechanisms: genericity applied to a statically type correct class must produce a statically type correct class.

7.1.2 Homogeneous Collections

Genericity is especially useful when programming "homogeneous" collections. A homogeneous collection class is a container class where we use a type annotation to limit what can be stored in its objects. Consider for example the container class from Section 5.6.3.

```
class Container
  var x
  method put(val)
    x := val;
    self
  end
  method get()
    x
  end
end
```

```
(Container new).put(7).get()+10;
(Container new).put(false).get() or true
```

This program yields no run-time errors. Still, as demonstrated in Section 5.6.3, it is necessary to duplicate the class Container before we (or a type inference algorithm) can annotate the program so that it is statically type correct. Clearly, the two annotated copies of the class will only differ at the places of type annotations. The challenge for genericity is to enable the programmer to conveniently specify this duplication together with the substitution of type annotations.

7.2   Previous Approaches

There have been several previous approaches to genericity. This section assesses the existing genericity mechanisms of parameterized classes, templates, and virtual binding.

7.2.1   EIFFEL: *Parameterized Classes*

The EIFFEL language was one of the first to feature the genericity mechanism of *parameterized classes*. For example, consider the following EIFFEL version of the Stack example from Chapter 2.

```
class Stack[T] export
  init, push, pop
feature
  s: array[T];
  high: Integer;

  Init is
  do high := 0
  end;
```

```
Push(x: T) is
do high := high+1;
   s(high) := x
end

Pop: T is
do high := high-1;
   Result := s(high+1)
end
end
```

In contrast to the previous version of Stack, the element type is a *parameter* T, rather than a class Element. In EIFFEL's typing rules, a type parameter works like a single token that is distinct from all others. Thus, a variable that is annotated with a type parameter can only be assigned other variables with that type.

To declare variables that can hold instances of Stack or subclasses of Stack, it is necessary to supply actual classes.

```
es: Stack [Element];
is: Stack [Integer];
```

The result is as if two versions of the Stack class had been written. This process is called *generic instantiation* of the parameterized class.

A parameterized class enables the substitution of type annotations because type parameters can be substituted by actual classes. Parameterized classes have several shortcomings, which in summary are:

- there are two kinds of classes;
- generic instantiation happens only once; and
- a generic instance is not a subclass.

The notion of class is useful in itself, also in the absence of inheritance. Inheritance can be added to any language with classes and it offers a convenient way of constructing new classes. No further concept than that of inheritance itself is needed when constructing new classes. The construct of parameterized classes, however, needs the auxiliary concept of type parameters to allow the substitution of type annotations. Thus, programmers are required to master both classes and parameterization. A programmer can construct a class without knowledge of inheritance, and yet the class can be inherited later on. In contrast, a programmer without knowledge of parameterization cannot construct a class which we can later generically instantiate. Also, it is unclear what the appropriate relationship between classes and parameterized classes should be.

When a parameterized class is generically instantiated, then the result is a class without type parameters. Of course, no further generic instantiation of the resulting class is possible. This property of parameterized classes can be illustrated as follows.

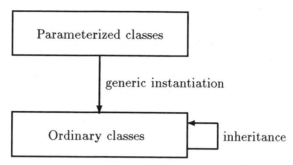

Thus, inheritance can be iterated, whereas generic instantiation cannot.

Inheritance yields subclasses; generic instantiation does not. This severely limits the available polymorphism. For example, it is not possible to write a method **DoublePop** that accepts as parameters objects of all generic instances of **Stack** to which the **Pop** message is then sent twice. In other words, we cannot define a type that consists of all generic instances of a parameterized class.

7.2.2   C++: Templates

The C++ language was in the late 1980s extended with the genericity mechanism of *templates*. A template is essentially a parameterized class. For example, consider the following C++ version of the **Stack** example from Chapter 2.

```
template <class T> class stack {
    T s[100];
    int high;
public:

    void Init() { high = 0; }

    void Push(T x) { s[++high] = x; }

    T Pop { s[high--]; }
}
```

Like in the EIFFEL version of this example, the element type is a *parameter* named T.

To declare variables that can hold instances of Stack or subclasses of Stack, it is necessary to first create generic instances, as in EIFFEL.

```
Stack<Element> es;
Stack<int> is;
```

The result is as if two versions of the Stack class had been written. Another possibility for using Stack is to explicitly create a new class, as follows.

```
Stack<complex> cs;
```

The comments on EIFFEL's parameterized classes also apply to templates.

7.2.3 BETA: Virtual Binding

The BETA language features the genericity mechanism of *virtual binding*. For example, consider the following BETA version of the Stack class from Chapter 2.

```
Stack: (#
    T:< Object;
    s: [100] @ T;
    high:@ Integer;

    Init: (# do 0 -> high #);

    Push: (#
            x :@ T;
            enter x;
            do high+1 -> high; x -> s[high];
    #);

    Pop: (#
            do high−1 -> high;
            exit s[high+1];
    #);
#);
```

The element type is a class, although a special one: this class is *virtually* bound. It is possible to construct a new class by so-called *extension* of the binding of T, as follows.

```
es: ElementStack : Stack (# T ::< Element #);
is: IntegerStack : Stack (# T ::< Integer #);
```

The extended binding must be to a subclass of what was previously bound. Thus, virtual bindings enable explicit substitution of type annotations.

Virtual binding does not have the three drawbacks of parameterized classes, since:

- no new class concept is needed;
- extended bindings can be extended again; and
- the extension of virtual bindings produces a subclass.

Virtual binding has a more subtle drawback, however. Consider the following BETA program.

```
C1: (# T:< Object;
        x:@ T;
        set: (# arg:@ T enter arg do arg -> x exit arg #);
     #);

C2: C1 (# T::< Integer #);

D1: (# S:< C1;
        c:@ S;
        p: (# r:@ Object enter r do r -> c.set #);
     #);

D2: D1 (# S::< C2 #);
```

The class C1 is clearly statically type correct and so is C2. To see that also the class D1 is statically type correct, notice that arg -> c.set assigns an instance of Object (namely r) to the enter part of set (namely arg) which is also of type object. Now, consider the class D2. This class is *not* statically type correct! This is because in D2 the type of the enter part of set is Integer (instead of Object), so the assignment in p is not statically type correct. Thus, in this case, the extension of virtual binding fails to preserve static type correctness. The situation can be further illustrated by the following exploded class graph, which clearly reveals the inconsistency.

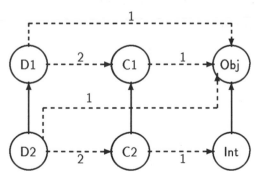

In the class D1 the **has-a** paths "1" and "2,1" lead to the same class, Object; however, in the subclass D2 they lead to two different classes, Object and Integer.

Both parameterized classes and virtual binding require explicit naming of the substitutable type annotations. In the remainder of this chapter we present a new genericity mechanism which is based on the idea of considering *all* type annotations to be substitutable.

7.3   Class Substitution

This section presents the genericity mechanism of *class substitution* and explains how it complements inheritance in a natural manner.

7.3.1   A New Subclassing Mechanism

Class substitution is a new genericity mechanism. It is designed to have the following properties.

All (transitive) has-a parts can be substituted.

Suppose a class C **has-a*** D. We can then construct a new class by substituting D with some other class. Notice that D does not have to appear in the text of C. For example, consider the following classes.

```
class C
   var a: X
end

class X
   var b: D
end
```

Clearly, C **has-a*** D, so with class substitution it is possible to produce a class similar to C, with D substituted by some other class.

No explicit type parameters.

Both parameterized classes and virtual binding require explicit naming of the substitutable type annotations. With class substitution, all type annotations are substitutable. This reduces to a minimum the amount of syntax needed for class substitution.

No new class concept.

Class substitution can be applied to all classes, just as inheritance can. Thus, a programmer can construct a class without knowledge of class substitution and yet apply class substitution to it later on. In contrast to virtual binding, nothing is specified in advance.

Class substitution can be repeated.

Like virtual binding, class substitution can be repeated. This means that we get the following scenario.

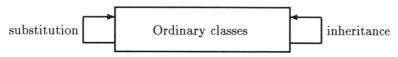

This picture directly reflects that genericity and inheritance are mechanisms for constructing new classes from existing ones.

Class substitution produces a subclass.

Like virtual binding, class substitution produces a subclass. Thus, the new class can reuse the compiled code of the existing class. This puts class substitution on an equal footing with inheritance. As discussed later, the run-time model for inheritance can also support class substitution.

Class substitution is orthogonal to inheritance.

Intuitively, genericity and inheritance are different: genericity changes invariants and inheritance changes behavior. With the introduction of class substitution, this intuition can be formalized: class substitution is *orthogonal* to inheritance, in a formal sense. We will later explain more about this.

Class substitution preserves static type correctness.

Earlier we mentioned the practical requirement that genericity applied to a statically type correct class must produce a statically type correct class. Class substitution meets this requirement.

7.3.2 Syntax

The basic syntax of class substitution in BOPL is as follows.

$$C[A_1, A_2, \ldots, A_n \leftarrow B_1, B_2, \ldots, B_n]$$

Intuitively, this results in a class like C where every A_i has been substituted by a subclass B_i. The requirement that each B_i is a subclass of A_i is necessary to ensure that the class substitution yields a subclass of C. The substitutions need not take place in the text of C itself. Consider for example the classes C and X from before:

```
class C
    var a: X
end

class X
    var b: D
end
```

If we here write $C[D \leftarrow E]$, then this evaluates to a class, say C', which looks as follows.

```
class C'
    var a: X'
end

class X'
    var b: E
end
```

To preserve static type correctness, it may be necessary to perform further substitutions. We shall later see how to do this in general. In BOPL, class substitution has the following syntax:

$$\text{CLASSEXP} \quad ::= \quad \text{ID} \mid \text{CLASSEXP} \; [\; \text{IDLIST} \leftarrow \text{IDLIST} \;]$$

The following syntax is the basic way of constructing a class using class substitution.

$$\text{CLASS} \qquad ::= \quad \textbf{class} \; \text{ID} \; \textbf{is} \; \text{CLASSEXP}$$

For example, consider the following class.

```
class List
    var head: Object
    var tail: List
end
```

Using class substitution, we can construct subclasses as follows.

```
class IntList is List[Object ← Int]
class BoolList is List[Object ← Bool]
class Matrix is List[Object ← IntList]
```

The syntax is much like generic instantiation of parameterized classes.

A class expression can be used everywhere a class name could be used before, that is, after **inherits** and **renews**, in types, in **new** expressions, and in **instance-of** expressions.

To summarize: class substitution is a genericity mechanism without the drawbacks of previous approaches to genericity. The precise meaning of class substitution will later be explained by means of an algorithm that *expands* class substitution.

7.3.3 Primitive Classes

Until now, we have had no reason to be concerned about whether Int and Bool are names of classes. Some languages are even a little ambivalent on this issue. We could for example follow the SMALLTALK approach of viewing primitive values as objects, and viewing the expression 8+7 as the object 8 receiving the message + with argument 7. We could also view primitive values as non-objects.

To enable some convenient substitutions we choose to view Int and Bool as classes. However, it is not possible to create subclasses of them. We shall also assume the existence of an empty class Object, which is a common superclass of all other classes, including Int and Bool. Thus, the complete class hierarchy in any BOPL program can be sketched as follows.

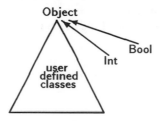

7.3.4 Examples

Class substitution is convenient. Consider for example the class hierarchy:

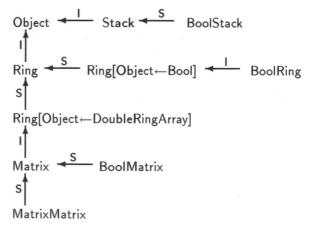

The symbol "I" indicates that the subclass has been constructed by inheritance; and the symbol "S" indicates that the subclass has been constructed by class substitution. For example we can obtain a stack of booleans by first programming a Stack where the element type is Object, and then substituting Object by Bool.

class BoolStack **is** Stack[Object ← Bool]

In the following we will present the code of the other classes. The example also includes the outline of the Array from Section 3.6.

```
class Array
    method at(i: Int) returns Object
    method atput(i: Int; x: Object) returns Array
    method initialize(size: Int) returns Array
    method arraysize() returns Int
end

class Ring
    var value: Object
    method plus(other: Ring) returns Ring
        self
    end
    method zero() returns Ring
        self
    end
    method getvalue() returns Object
        value
    end
end

class BoolRing inherits Ring[Object ← Bool]
    method plus(other: BoolRing) returns BoolRing
        value := value or (other.getvalue());
        self
    end
    method zero() returns BoolRing
        value := false;
        self
    end
end

class RingArray is Array[Object ← Ring]
```

```
class DoubleArray is Array[Object ← Array]

class DoubleRingArray is DoubleArray[Object ← Ring]

class Matrix inherits Ring[Object ← DoubleRingArray]
    var i, j: Int
    var r: RingArray
    method plus(other: Matrix) returns Matrix
      i := 0;
      while i<value.arraysize() do
        r := value.at(i);
        j := 0;
        while j<r.arraysize() do
          r := r.atput(j, r.at(j).plus(other.at(i).at(j)));
          j := j+1
        end;
        value.atput(i, r);
        i := i+1
      end;
      self
    end
    method zero() returns Matrix
      i := 0;
      while i<value.arraysize() do
        r := value.at(i);
        j := 0;
        while j<r.arraysize() do
          r := r.atput(j, r.at(j).zero());
          j := j+1
        end;
        value.atput(i, r);
        i := i+1
      end;
      self
    end
end

class BoolMatrix is Matrix[Ring ← BoolRing]

class MatrixMatrix is Matrix[Ring ← Matrix]
```

Note that the class MatrixMatrix implements matrices whose elements themselves are matrices.

It is an illustrative exercise to program a similar hierarchy using either parameterized classes or virtual bindings. In the former case, it requires considerable foresight to provide the appropriate parameters, and—depending on what the language allows—it may be problematic to obtain the required subclass relationships. In the latter case, it is necessary to introduce numerous temporary classes and to explicitly extend cascades of virtual bindings, in order to preserve static type correctness.

7.3.5   Orthogonality to Inheritance

Class substitution is orthogonal to inheritance. In the bibliographical notes to this chapter we refer to results establishing this in a formal sense. Here, we will concentrate on the intuitive and practical contents of this result.

The idea is to consider all possible subclass relationships that can be produced by class substitution and inheritance, respectively. This yields two partial orders that are *orthogonal*, in a sense analogous to the concept for vector spaces.

- If a class D can be obtained from C by inheritance, then D *cannot* be obtained from C by class substitution; and
- If a class D can be obtained from C by class substitution, then D *cannot* be obtained from C by inheritance.

Thus, we can think of class substitution and inheritance as two orthogonal mechanisms that together span the possible subclasses of any given class. This can be illustrated as follows.

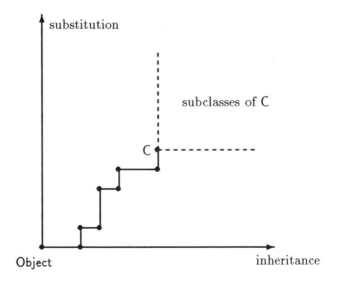

7.3.6   Beyond Textual Substitution

When actual type parameters are supplied to a parameterized class, then conceptually a textual substitution takes place. Similarly, when a virtual binding is extended, we can think of it as a textual substitution.

Class substitution is different. In contrast to virtual binding, class substitution preserves static type correctness. In order to do that, class substitution may yield *more* individual substitutions than those explicitly specified.

For example, consider the following BOPL version of four classes that we have previously seen programmed in BETA.

```
class C1
    var x: Object
    method set(arg: Object) returns Object
        x := arg
    end
end

class C2 is C1[Object ← Int]

class D1
    var c: C1
    method p(r: Object) returns Object
        c.set(r)
    end
end

class D2 is D1[C1 ← C2]
```

A direct definition of C2 should of course be as follows.

```
class C2
    var x: Int
    method set(arg: Int) returns Int
        x := arg
    end
end
```

This is indeed what is produced by the substitution expansion algorithm that we present later. It is also, however, the result of textually substituting Object by Int in the text of C1. Consider then textually substituting C1 by C2 in the text of D1. We obtain:

```
class D2
  var c: C2
  method p(r: Object) returns Object
    c.set(r)
  end
end
```

This is exactly the situation we analyzed in connection with the corresponding BETA program. The point is that this class is *not* statically correct. This is because the argument r of type Object is passed to a method set where the formal parameter is of type Int. Thus, textual substitution does not preserve static type correctness.

Class substitution manages to preserve static type correctness by performing *derived* substitutions. In the case of D2, class substitution detects that substituting C1 by C2 really implies also substituting Object by Int. This information can be systematically computed by comparing the type annotations of C1 and C2. In the following section we fully develop this intuition and gives an algorithm for expanding away class substitutions. The expansion of D2 yielded by this algorithm is:

```
class D2
  var c: C2
  method p(r: Int) returns Int
    c.set(r)
  end
end
```

This class is clearly statically type correct.

7.3.7 Avoiding Substitution

In some situations, class substitution may be too eager in performing substitutions. Consider for example the task of programming a class of finite maps. A first approximation could look as follows.

```
class Map
  var arg, res: Object
  var next: Map
  method Update(a, r: Object) returns Map
    . . .
  end
  method Lookup(a: Object) returns Object
    . . .
  end
end
```

We have chosen **Object** as the type of both arguments and results, because we want to be able to use class substitution to obtain maps between arbitrary classes. However, in order to guarantee static type correctness, all occurrences of **Object** must be substituted by the *same* subclass. Thus, we are unable to create for example a map from integers to booleans.

The solution has already been introduced, since we can simply use the idea of class renewal and multiple tokens suggested in Section 6.3.4. If we employ two different tokens for **Object**, then we guarantee that they can never be confused. In return, we are allowed to perform independent substitutions. Hence, a proper implementation of maps is as follows.

> **class** Argument **renews** Object
> **class** Result **renews** Object
>
> **class** Map
>   **var** arg: Argument
>   **var** res: Result
>   **var** next: Map
>   **method** Update(a: Argument ; r: Result) **returns** Map
>   ...
>   **end**
>   **method** Lookup(a: Argument) **returns** Result
>   ...
>   **end**
> **end**

Now, we can define a map from integers to booleans as follows.

> **class** IBMap **is** Map[Argument, Result $\leftarrow$ Int, Bool]

In this case, the use of multiple tokens improves the readability.

7.4 The Substitution Expansion Algorithm

This section shows how to explain class substitution as expansion of source code, similarly to the technique used for inheritance.

7.4.1 *Well-Formedness*

First we must find an appropriate order in which to expand the classes. The following two sections explain how to expand *individual* ones. Consider a class expressions of the following form.

$$C[A_{1i} \leftarrow B_{1i}] \ldots [A_{nj} \leftarrow B_{nj}]$$

It can be simplified by the creation of fresh classes $F_1, \ldots, F_n$ as follows.

    class F_1 **is** $C[A_{1i} \leftarrow B_{1i}]$

    $\vdots$

    class F_n **is** $F_{n-1}[A_{ni} \leftarrow B_{ni}]$

We can then replace the entire class expression:

    $C[A_{1i} \leftarrow B_{1i}] \ldots [A_{ni} \leftarrow B_{ni}]$

by the class name F_n. After this simplification, all class substitutions in the program occur in class definitions of the form:

    class F **is** $C[A_1, A_2, \ldots, A_n \leftarrow B_1, B_2, \ldots, B_n]$

where we can assume that C is a class name.

We can only proceed if the program is *well-formed*, which is defined similarly to the criterion for inheritance. We introduce a binary **uses-a** relation which indicates substitution dependencies. They supplement the **is-a** relation. In the above example, we have that F **is-a** C, F **uses-a** A_i, and F **uses-a** B_i.

Well-formedness is now the property that no cycle in the class graph contains an **is-a** or a **uses-a** edge. Like before, the relation $X \leq Y$ on classes holds if $X=Y$ or there is a path from Y to X containing at least one **is-a** or **uses-a** edge. Because of well-formedness, this is a partial order, and we shall process classes topologically sorted according to $\leq$.

An ordinary class implementation does not involve class substitution and requires no further processing. We are now left with the problem of expanding a class substitution

    $C[A_1, A_2, \ldots, A_n \leftarrow B_1, B_2, \ldots, B_n]$

where, due to well-formedness, we can assume that C, A_i, and B_i are classes *without* class substitutions. We will present the algorithm for doing that in two steps. First, we consider the simpler case of $n = 1$. Afterwards, we show a straightforward extension of the technique that treats the general case.

7.4.2 Single Substitutions

Consider the class substitution:

    $C[A \leftarrow B]$

where C, A, and B are classes *without* class substitutions. The algorithm for expanding this is recursive and uses a consistent, exploded class graph as global data. The exploded class graph must have a path of zero or more **is-a** edges from B to A; otherwise, the specification is rejected by the compiler.

Initially, a copy of C named C'A←B is created with an **is-a** edge to C. We then compute from A and B a partial *substitution map*, denoted sᴜʙ(A,B), which is defined as follows. Assume that A contains a sequence of **has-a** edges leading to a class A'. From consistency, we know that from B we can follow a **has-a** path with the same labels, leading to a class B'. Consistency also implies that there is an **is-a** edge from B' to A'. The situation is illustrated as follows.

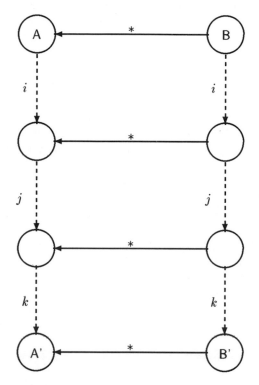

Now, for all such situations, sᴜʙ(A,B) maps A' to B'. The implementation of C'A←B is a copy of C's implementation subjected to the following change of every **has-a** occurrence of a class X.

- If X is in the domain of sᴜʙ(A,B), then it is replaced by sᴜʙ(A,B)(X).
- Otherwise, if X'A←B is already present in the class graph, then X is replaced by this class.
- If not, then X is replaced by the result of recursively expanding X[A ← B].

The above algorithm clearly terminates, since only finitely many triples of the form C'A←B exist. The resulting exploded class graph will still be consistent, since sᴜʙ(A,B) is a *map* with **is-a** edges to every argument from its result.

7.4.3 Multiple Substitutions

We are now ready to treat the general case of the class substitution:

$$C[A_1, A_2, \ldots, A_n \leftarrow B_1, B_2, \ldots, B_n]$$

where we can assume that C, A_i, and B_i are classes *without* class substitutions.

The technique is identical to the one previously described, except that we now get n substitution maps, each of the form $\mathrm{SUB}(A_i, B_i)$. Each pair of these maps must agree on their common domain; otherwise, the specification is rejected by the compiler. We then simply proceed using a substitution map that is the union of the n individual ones.

7.4.4 Type Correctness of Subclasses

It was argued above that the exploded class graph remained consistent after expansion of class substitution. From the discussion in Section 6.4.4, we can then conclude that class substitution also preserves static correctness of subclasses.

7.5   The Run-Time Model for Substitution

When class substitution is applied, then arguments of **new** and **instance-of** may change. In this section we observe that the technique of instantiator lookup that was introduced in the run-time model for inheritance is sufficient to handle these changes. Thus, the compiled code for a class can be reused for all its subclasses obtained by substitution. We illustrate this with the following simple example.

```
class A                          class D1
    var a                            var x
end                                  method n()
                                         x := (C1 new);
                                         x := x.m()
class B inherits A                       x instance-of A
    var b                            end
end                              end

class C1                         class D2 is D1[C1 ← C2]
    method m()
        A new
    end
end

class C2 is C1[A ← B]
```

They expand into these classes.

```
class A                          class D1
    var a                            var x
end                                  method n()
                                         x := (C1 new);
class B                                  x := x.m()
    var a,b                              x instance-of A
end                                  end
                                 end
class C1
    method m()                   class D2
        A new                        var x
    end                              method n()
end                                      x := (C2 new);
                                         x := x.m()
class C2                                 x instance-of B
    method m()                       end
        B new                    end
    end
end
```

At run-time, the code space looks as follows.

```
512: push allocate(l-lookup(class(self),w₁))
     return
  ⋮
607: push allocate(l-lookup(class(self),w₂))
     assign x
     call M-lookup(class(x),m)
     assign x
     if class(x)≠l-lookup(class(self),w₃) then run-time-error
     return
```

It goes together with these six class descriptors.

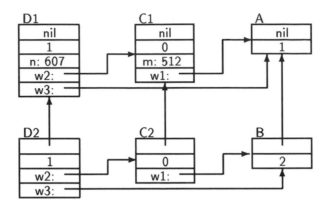

Notice how subclasses formed by either inheritance or substitution are uniformly represented at run-time.

7.6   Class Types

So far, we have considered class substitution under a closed-world assumption. We will now sketch how to integrate class substitution into a language with class types.

Suppose we remove parameterized classes from EIFFEL, remove templates from C++, and remove virtual binding from BETA. Instead, we introduce syntax for class substitution.

The key to giving meaning to class substitutions is to redefine **has-a**. If the class type ↑C appears in the text of a class X, then X **has-a** C. Notice that the **has-a** relationship only applies to the root of the cone.

We can then use the same definition of the substitution map. When applying the substitution map, it should only be applied to the root of the cones. The reader may check that this yields the desired result for the program in Section 7.2.6, assuming that the types in that program are interpreted as class types.

Bibliographical Notes

Genericity constructs are found in some imperative languages. Major examples are the generic packages of ADA [24] and the parameterized CLU clusters [41].

A comparison of inheritance and parameterized classes was presented by Meyer [44]. A presentation of the virtual classes in BETA can be found in [43].

Ohori and Buneman [48] presented a type inference algorithm for a functional language featuring parameterized classes.

The type system of EIFFEL does not entirely guarantee safety. Cook [17] presented several EIFFEL programs demonstrating this and suggested various improvements to the type system.

The mechanism of class substitution was first presented in [54]. A proof of inheritance and class substitution being orthogonal is given in [53].

Exercises

1. Extend the syntax of BOPL with simple parameterized classes and generic instantiation. Show how to generate the appropriate type constraints. Argue that generic instantiation will preserve static type correctness.
2. Sketch what Int and Bool would look like if they were truly implemented as typed classes in BOPL.
3. Consider the matrix classes in Section 7.3.4. Show how to program a class of matrices whose elements are boolean matrices. How should a class MatrixMatrixMatrix be programmed, and what would it implement?
4. Implement the class hierarchy in Section 7.3.4 using:

   a) parameterized classes
   b) virtual binding

5. Consider the claim of orthogonality in Section 7.3.5. Show that if a class D can be obtained from a class C by *both* inheritance and substitution, then it must be the case that C=D.
6. Give a practical example where it is necessary to renew classes different from Object.
7. Regard the classes U, V, W, and R from Section 6.3.3. We wish to create a new class:

   class T **is** R[V ← R]

   Run the substitution expansion algorithm. Draw the resulting exploded class graph and verify that it is consistent.
8. Show the run-time representation of the class hierarchy from Section 7.3.4.
9. Consider the following classes.

```
class Even
    var eventail: Odd
    method Tail( ) returns Odd
        eventail
    end
end
```

```
class Odd
    var oddtail: Even
    method Tail() returns Even
        oddtail
    end
end

class ColorEven inherits Even
    var color: Int
    method SetColor(c: Int) returns Int
        color := c
    end
end
```

In some other class we find the following variable declarations and expression.

```
var x: ColorEven
var y: ??


y := x.Tail().Tail().Tail() ;
y.Tail().SetColor(4)
```

Annotate y so that the expression is statically type correct (hint: use class substitution). How can it be done with parameterized classes or virtual binding, perhaps with some changes in the program text?

10. Suppose we allow a class to be substituted by any other class, not only subclasses. Write classes A, B, and C where A **has-a** B so that A is statically type correct but A[B←C] is not.

11. Write classes A, B, C, D, and E so that the expanded versions of A[B,C←D,E] and A[B←D][C←A] are different.

12. What is the worst-case running time of the substitution expansion algorithm?

13. Sketch how the transformation in Section 7.4.1 affects the class graph.

14. Consider the following classes.

```
class A
    var a: Object
end

class B inherits A
    var b: Int
end
```

```
class C
    var c: A
end

class X is C [A ← B]

class D inherits X
    var d: Object
end

class E
    var e: C
end
```

First, draw the class graph and expand away inheritance. Then, expand the class expression E[C,Object←D,Bool].

15. Suppose we, following Section 7.6, introduce class substitution into a language with class types. Consider an assignment:

```
var a: ↑C
var b: ↑D
```

```
a := b
```

Under which conditions on C and D will the assignment be statically type correct in all subclasses?

16. Our algorithms for expanding inheritance and substitution are supposed to be executed in the following order: first expand inheritance, then substitution. Explain the difficulties involved in designing algorithms for doing expansions in the reverse order. Which parts of the present substitution expansion algorithm can be executed before the present inheritance expansion algorithm?

A

The BOPL Grammar

The BOPL language has eight variations: the basic one and seven extensions with type annotations, inheritance, and genericity. Here is again the overview table from chapter 1:

		Inheritance	*Genericity*	*Inheritance+Genericity*
Untyped	BOPL	IBOPL	SBOPL	ISBOPL
Typed	TBOPL	ITBOPL	STBOPL	ISTBOPL

All BOPL programs are also TBOPL programs; all IBOPL programs are also ISTBOPL programs, and so on. In the following we present the grammar of the biggest language, ISTBOPL. Some of the productions are labeled with TBOPL, IBOPL, SBOPL, or ISBOPL. All other constructs are part of all languages, including BOPL. The idea with the labels is that for a given program, one can find out which of the labeled constructs are used, and then deduce the minimal language to which the program belongs. For example, if a program contains constructs labeled TBOPL and SBOPL, then the program belongs to STBOPL, and thus also to ISTBOPL. The inclusions among the languages can be illustrated as follows:

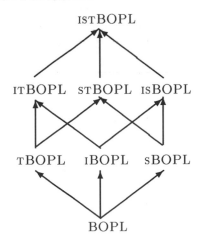

Here follows the IST BOPL grammar:

```
PROGRAM            ::=  CLASSLIST? EXP

CLASSLIST?         ::=  ε | CLASSLIST
CLASSLIST          ::=  CLASS | CLASSLIST CLASS

CLASS              ::=  class ID VARLIST? METHODLIST? end |
                       class ID inherits CLASSEXP
                           VARLIST? METHODLIST?
                       end |                              IBOPL
                       class ID is CLASSEXP |
                       class ID renews CLASSEXP           ISBOPL

CLASSEXP           ::=  Int | Bool | ID |
                       CLASSEXP [ IDLIST ← IDLIST ]       SBOPL
CLASSEXPLIST?      ::=  ε | CLASSEXPLIST
CLASSEXPLIST       ::=  CLASSEXP | CLASSEXPLIST , CLASSEXP
METHODLIST?        ::=  ε | METHODLIST
METHODLIST         ::=  METHOD | METHODLIST METHOD
METHOD             ::=  method ID FORMALS RETURNTYPE
                           EXP
                       end

VARLIST?           ::=  ε | VARLIST
VARLIST            ::=  VAR | VARLIST VAR
VAR                ::=  var DEC

FORMALS            ::=  ( DECLIST? )
DECLIST?           ::=  ε | DECLIST
DECLIST            ::=  DEC | DECLIST ; DEC
DEC                ::=  IDLIST : TYPE |                    TBOPL
                       IDLIST
IDLIST             ::=  ID | IDLIST , ID
TYPE               ::=  CLASSEXP | { CLASSEXPLIST? }
RETURNTYPE         ::=  ε |
                       returns TYPE                        TBOPL

EXP                ::=  INT |
                       EXP BINOP EXP |
                       false |
                       true |
                       EXP not |
```

```
                         ID := EXP |
                         EXP ; EXP |
                         if EXP then EXP else EXP end |
                         while EXP do EXP end |
                         nil |
                         self |
                         super |                              ιBOPL
                         CLASSEXP new |
                         EXP class new |
                         EXP instance-of TYPE |
                         ID |
                         EXP . ID ( EXPLIST? ) |
                         ( EXP )
BINOP            ::=  + | - | * | = | and | or | <
EXPLIST?         ::=  ε | EXPLIST
EXPLIST          ::=  EXP | EXPLIST , EXP

INT              ::=  DIGIT | DIGIT INT
DIGIT            ::=  0 | 1 | 2 | 3 | 4 | 5 | 6 | 7 | 8 | 9
ID               ::=  LETTER | ID LETTER | ID DIGIT
LETTER           ::=  a | b | ... | z | A | B | ... | Z
```

Thus, there are six constructs that are not part of BOPL but part of some extensions: inheritance, **renews**, substitution, type annotations, return types, and **super**.

B

The Workbench

The algorithms presented in this book are implemented in a freely available workbench. This appendix explains how to get it and how to use it.

How to get it

The workbench can be obtained by anonymous *ftp* from the machine:

daimi.aau.dk   (130.225.16.1)

in the directory:

pub/oots/workbench

Get all the files in this directory and follow the set-up instructions in the README file.

How to use it

To run the workbench, type:

bopl

This starts a Unix-like "shell". For example, if the file prog1 contains an ASCII version of an IST BOPL program, then the command:

prog1 | iexpand | erase | sexpand

will transform the program into a BOPL program and then execute it. If the file prog2 contains a BOPL program, then the command:

prog2 | infer | check > prog3

will infer type annotations, ensure static type correctness, and place an ASCII version of the resulting program on the file prog3 and also place a LaTeX version on the file prog3.tex.

All the program examples in this book have been generated using the workbench. The example programs are contained in the above directory.

The possible commands are erase, iexpand, sexpand, check, infer, ct, mt, and extract.

- erase. Deletes type annotations.
- iexpand. Transforms a program into one that does not use inheritance.
- sexpand. Transforms a program into one that does not use substitution.
- check. Type checks a program. This may involve inserting dynamic type checks and lead to rejection of the program.
- infer. Inserts type annotations.
- ct. Transforms an untyped program by copying classes.
- mt. Transforms an untyped program by copying methods.
- extract. Removes dead code.

A command line can be of two forms:

- infile | command$_1$ | ... | command$_n$
- infile | command$_1$ | ... | command$_n$ > outfile

In both cases, each of the commands 1–n are executed in turn. In the first case, the resulting program is executed. In the second case, the resulting program is placed on outfile and outfile.tex.

Suppose the file prog1 contains an IBOPL program and that we type the line:

prog1 | infer

The type inference algorithm is only defined for BOPL programs, but instead of rejecting the line, the workbench understands the line as an abbreviation for:

prog1 | iexpand | infer

Thus, the inheritance is expanded away before the type inference takes place. Similar remarks applies to the other commands: if a command cannot directly be executed, then appropriate transformations are automatically inserted.

References

[1] Ole Agesen, Lars Bak, Craig Chambers, Bay-Wei Chang, Urs Hölzle, John Maloney, Randall B. Smith, and David Ungar. The SELF programmer's reference manual. Technical report, Sun Microsystems, Inc, 2550 Garcia Avenue, Mountain View, CA 94043, USA, 1992. Version 2.0.

[2] Ole Agesen, Jens Palsberg, and Michael I. Schwartzbach. Type inference of Self: Analysis of objects with dynamic and multiple inheritance. In *Proc. ECOOP'93, Seventh European Conference on Object-Oriented Programming*, Kaiserslautern, Germany, July 1993. To appear.

[3] Paul Bergstein. Object-preserving class transformations. In *Proc. OOPSLA'91, ACM SIGPLAN Sixth Annual Conference on Object-Oriented Programming Systems, Languages and Applications*, pages 299–313, 1991.

[4] Alan H. Borning. Classes versus prototypes in object-oriented languages. In *ACM/IEEE Fall Joint Computer Conference*, pages 36–40, 1986.

[5] Alan H. Borning and Daniel H. H. Ingalls. A type declaration and inference system for Smalltalk. In *Ninth Symposium on Principles of Programming Languages*, pages 133–141. ACM Press, January 1982.

[6] Gilad Bracha and William Cook. Mixin-based inheritance. In *Proc. OOPSLA/ECOOP'90, ACM SIGPLAN Fifth Annual Conference on Object-Oriented Programming Systems, Languages and Applications; European Conference on Object-Oriented Programming*, pages 303–311, 1990.

[7] Kim B. Bruce and Giuseppe Longo. A modest model of records, inheritance, and bounded quatification. *Information and Computation*, 87:196–240, 1990.

[8] Peter S. Canning, William R. Cook, Walter L. Hill, John Mitchell, and Walter G. Olthoff. F-bounded polymorphism for object-oriented

programming. In *Proc. Conference on Functional Programming Languages and Computer Architecture*, pages 273–280, 1989.

[9] L. Cardelli, J. C. Mitchell, S. Martini, and A. Scedrov. An extension of system F with subtyping. In *Proc. TACS'91*, 1991.

[10] Luca Cardelli. A semantics of multiple inheritance. In Gilles Kahn, David MacQueen, and Gordon Plotkin, editors, *Semantics of Data Types*, pages 51–68. Springer-Verlag (*LNCS* 173), 1984.

[11] Luca Cardelli and John C. Mitchell. Operations on records. In *Proc. Mathmatical Foundations of Programming Semantics*, pages 22–52. Springer-Verlag (*LNCS* 442), 1989.

[12] Luca Cardelli and Peter Wegner. On understanding types, data abstraction, and polymorphism. *ACM Computing Surveys*, 17(4):471–522, December 1985.

[13] Eduardo Casais. An incremental class reorganization approach. In *Proc. ECOOP'92, Sixth European Conference on Object-Oriented Programming*, pages 114–132. Springer-Verlag (*LNCS* 615), July 1992.

[14] William Cook, Walter Hill, and Peter Canning. Inheritance is not subtyping. In *Seventeenth Symposium on Principles of Programming Languages*, pages 125–135. ACM Press, January 1990.

[15] William Cook and Jens Palsberg. A denotational semantics of inheritance and its correctness. *Information and Computation*. To appear. Also in Proc. OOPSLA'89, ACM SIGPLAN Fourth Annual Conference on Object-Oriented Programming Systems, Languages and Applications, pages 433–443, New Orleans, Louisiana, October 1989.

[16] William R. Cook. *A Denotational Semantics of Inheritance*. PhD thesis, Brown University, 1989.

[17] William R. Cook. A proposal for making Eiffel type-safe. *The Computer Journal*, 32(4):305–311, 1989.

[18] William R. Cook. Interfaces and specifications for the Smalltalk-80 collection classes. In *Proc. OOPSLA'92, ACM SIGPLAN Seventh Annual Conference on Object-Oriented Programming Systems, Languages and Applications*, pages 1–15, 1992.

[19] Brad J. Cox. *Object Oriented Programming, an Evolutionary Approach*. Addison-Wesley Publishing Company, 1986.

[20] Ole-Johan Dahl, Bjørn Myhrhaug, and Kristen Nygaard. Simula 67 common base language. Technical report, Norwegian Computing Center, Oslo, Norway, 1968.

[21] Ole-Johan Dahl and Kristen Nygaard. Simula—an Algol-based simulation language. *Communications of the ACM*, 9(9):671–678, September 1966.

[22] Scott Danforth and Chris Tomlinson. Type theories and object-oriented programming. *ACM Computing Surveys*, 20(1):29–72, March 1988.

[23] Margaret A. Ellis and Bjarne Stroustrup. *The Annotated* C++ *Reference Manual.* Addison-Wesley, 1990.

[24] Jean D. Ichbiah et al. *Reference Manual for the Ada Programming Language.* US DoD, July 1982.

[25] Giorgio Ghelli. A static type system for message passing. In *Proc. OOPSLA'91, ACM SIGPLAN Sixth Annual Conference on Object-Oriented Programming Systems, Languages and Applications*, pages 129–145, 1991.

[26] Adele Goldberg and David Robson. *Smalltalk-80—The Language and its Implementation.* Addison-Wesley, 1983.

[27] Justin O. Graver and Ralph E. Johnson. A type system for Smalltalk. In *Seventeenth Symposium on Principles of Programming Languages*, pages 136–150. ACM Press, January 1990.

[28] Justin Owen Graver. *Type-Checking and Type-Inference for Object-Oriented Programming Languages.* PhD thesis, Department of Computer Science, University of Illinois at Urbana-Champaign, August 1989. UIUCD-R-89-1539.

[29] Daniel C. Halbert and Patrick D. O'Brian. Using types and inheritance in object-oriented programming. *IEEE Software*, September 1987.

[30] Andreas V. Hense. Polymorphic type inference for a simple object oriented programming language with state. Technical Report No. A 20/90, Fachbericht 14, Universität des Saarlandes, December 1990.

[31] Andreas V. Hense. Wrapper semantics of an object-oriented programming language with state. In T. Ito and A. R. Meyer, editors, *Proc. Theoretical Aspects of Computer Software*, pages 548–568. Springer-Verlag (*LNCS* 526), 1991.

[32] Urs Hölzle, Craig Chambers, and David Ungar. Optimizing dynamically-typed object-oriented languages with polymorphic inline caches. In *Proc. ECOOP'91, Fifth European Conference on Object-Oriented Programming*, pages 21–38, 1991.

[33] Jin Ho Hur and Kilnam Chon. Self and selftype. *Information Processing Letters*, 36:225–230, 1990.

[34] Ralph E. Johnson. Type-checking Smalltalk. In *Proc. OOPSLA'86, Object-Oriented Programming Systems, Languages and Applications*, pages 315–321. Sigplan Notices, 21(11), November 1986.

[35] Samuel Kamin. Inheritance in Smalltalk–80: A denotational definition. In *Fifteenth Symposium on Principles of Programming Languages*, pages 80–87. ACM Press, January 1988.

[36] Jørgen Lindskov Knudsen and Ole Lehrmann Madsen. Teaching object-oriented programming is more than teaching object-oriented programming languages. In *Proc. ECOOP'88, European Conference on Object-Oriented Programming*, pages 21–40. Springer-Verlag (*LNCS* 322), 1988.

[37] Dexter Kozen, Jens Palsberg, and Michael I. Schwartzbach. Efficient inference of partial types. *Journal of Computer and System Sciences*. To appear. Also in Proc. FOCS'92, 33rd IEEE Symposium on Foundations of Computer Science, pages 363–371, Pittsburgh, Pennsylvania, October 1992.

[38] Bent B. Kristensen, Ole Lehrmann Madsen, Birger Møller-Pedersen, and Kristen Nygaard. The BETA programming language. In Bruce Shriver and Peter Wegner, editors, *Research Directions in Object-Oriented Programming*, pages 7–48. MIT Press, 1987.

[39] Karl Lieberherr, Paul Bergstein, and Nacho Silva-Lepe. From objects to classes: algorithms for optimal object-oriented design. *Journal of Software Engineering*, July 1991.

[40] Henry Lieberman. Using prototypical objects to implement shared behavior in object-oriented systems. In *Proc. OOPSLA'86, Object-Oriented Programming Systems, Languages and Applications*, pages 214–223. Sigplan Notices, 21(11), November 1986.

[41] Barbara Liskov, Alan Snyder, Russell Atkinson, and Craig Scaffert. Abstraction mechanisms in CLU. *Communications of the ACM*, 20(8):564–576, August 1977.

[42] Ole Lehrmann Madsen, Boris Magnusson, and Birger Møller-Pedersen. Strong typing of object-oriented languages revisited. In *Proc. OOPSLA/ECOOP'90, ACM SIGPLAN Fifth Annual Conference on Object-Oriented Programming Systems, Languages and Applications; European Conference on Object-Oriented Programming*, pages 140–150, 1990.

[43] Ole Lehrmann Madsen and Birger Møller-Pedersen. Virtual classes: A powerful mechanism in object-oriented programming. In *Proc. OOPSLA'89, Fourth Annual Conference on Object-Oriented Programming Systems, Languages and Applications*, pages 397–406. ACM, 1989.

[44] Bertrand Meyer. Genericity versus inheritance. *Journal of Pascal, Ada, and Modula-2*, 7(2):13–30, 1988.

[45] Bertrand Meyer. *Object-Oriented Software Construction*. Prentice-Hall, Englewood Cliffs, NJ, 1988.

[46] Flemming Nielson and Hanne Riis Nielson. *Two-Level Functional Languages*. Cambridge University Press, 1992.

[47] Hanne R. Nielson and Flemming Nielson. Transformations on higher-order functions. In *Proc. Conference on Functional Programming Languages and Computer Architecture*, pages 129–143, 1989.

[48] Atsushi Ohori and Peter Buneman. Static type inference for parametric classes. In *Proc. OOPSLA'89, Fourth Annual Conference on Object-Oriented Programming Systems, Languages and Applications*, pages 445–456. ACM, 1989.

[49] Patrick M. O'Keefe and Mitchell Wand. Type inference for partial types is decidable. In *Proc. ESOP'92, European Symposium on Programming*, pages 408–417. Springer-Verlag (*LNCS* 582), 1992.

[50] Nicholas Oxhøj, Jens Palsberg, and Michael I. Schwartzbach. Making type inference practical. In *Proc. ECOOP'92, Sixth European Conference on Object-Oriented Programming*, pages 329–349. Springer-Verlag (*LNCS* 615), Utrecht, The Netherlands, July 1992.

[51] Jens Palsberg. Normal forms have partial types. *Information Processing Letters*, 45:1–3, 1993.

[52] Jens Palsberg and Michael I. Schwartzbach. Safety analysis versus type inference. Submitted for publication.

[53] Jens Palsberg and Michael I. Schwartzbach. Static typing for object-oriented programming. *Science of Computer Programming*. To appear.

[54] Jens Palsberg and Michael I. Schwartzbach. Type substitution for object-oriented programming. In *Proc. OOPSLA/ECOOP'90, ACM SIGPLAN Fifth Annual Conference on Object-Oriented Programming Systems, Languages and Applications; European Conference on Object-Oriented Programming*, pages 151–160, Ottawa, Canada, October 1990.

[55] Jens Palsberg and Michael I. Schwartzbach. Object-oriented type inference. In *Proc. OOPSLA'91, ACM SIGPLAN Sixth Annual Conference on Object-Oriented Programming Systems, Languages and Applications*, pages 146–161, Phoenix, Arizona, October 1991.

[56] Jens Palsberg and Michael I. Schwartzbach. What is type-safe code reuse? In *Proc. ECOOP'91, Fifth European Conference on Object-Oriented Programming*, pages 325–341. Springer-Verlag (*LNCS* 512), Geneva, Switzerland, July 1991.

[57] Jens Palsberg and Michael I. Schwartzbach. Safety analysis versus type inference for partial types. *Information Processing Letters*, 43:175–180, 1992.

[58] Benjamin C. Pierce. Bounded quantification is undecidable. In *Nineteenth Annual ACM SIGACT-SIGPLAN Symposium on Principles of Programming Languages. Albuquerque, New Mexico*, pages 305–315, January 1992.

[59] Uday S. Reddy. Objects as closures: Abstract semantics of object-oriented languages. In *Proc. ACM Conference on Lisp and Functional Programming*, pages 289–297, 1988.

[60] Markku Sakkinen. Selftype is a special case. *Information Processing Letters*, 38:221–224, 1991.

[61] Michael I. Schwartzbach. Type inference with inequalities. In *Proc. TAPSOFT'91*, pages 441–455. Springer-Verlag (*LNCS* 493), 1991.

[62] Alan Snyder. Inheritance and the development of encapsulated software components. In Bruce Shriver and Peter Wegner, editors, *Research Directions in Object-Oriented Programming*, pages 165–188. MIT Press, 1987.

[63] Bjarne Stroustrup. *The C++ Programming Language*. Addison-Wesley, 1986.

[64] Bjarne Stroustrup. A history of C++: 1979–1991. Manuscript, 1993.

[65] Norihisa Suzuki. Inferring types in Smalltalk. In *Eighth Symposium on Principles of Programming Languages*, pages 187–199. ACM Press, January 1981.

[66] Satish Thatte. Type inference with partial types. In *Proc. International Colloquium on Automata, Languages, and Programming 1988*, pages 615–629. Springer-Verlag (*LNCS* 317), 1988.

[67] David Ungar and Randall B. Smith. SELF: The power of simplicity. In *Proc. OOPSLA'87, Object-Oriented Programming Systems, Languages and Applications*, pages 227–241, 1987. Also published in Lisp and Symbolic Computation 4(3), Kluwer Acadamic Publishers, June, 1991.

[68] Jan Vitek, R. Nigel Horspool, and James S. Uhl. Compile-time analysis of object-oriented programs. In *Proc. CC'92, 4th International Conference on Compiler Construction, Paderborn, Germany*, pages 236–250. Springer-Verlag (*LNCS* 641), 1992.

[69] Mitchell Wand. A simple algorithm and proof for type inference. *Fundamentae Informaticae*, X:115–122, 1987.

[70] Mitchell Wand and Patrick M. O'Keefe. Partially typed terms are strongly normalizing. Manuscript, December 1991.

[71] Peter Wegner. Dimensions of object-based language design. In *Proc. OOPSLA'87, Object-Oriented Programming Systems, Languages and Applications*, pages 168–182, 1987.

[72] Peter Wegner and Stanley B. Zdonik. Inheritance as an incremental modification mechanism or what like is and isn't like. In *Proc. ECOOP'88, European Conference on Object-Oriented Programming*, pages 55–77. Springer-Verlag (*LNCS* 322), 1988.

Index